CHURCHILL

by

Martin Gilbert

CHANCELLOR PRESS

First published in Great Britain by Park Lane Press
and distributed by Marks & Spencers Ltd

This edition published in 1983 by Chancellor Press
59 Grosvenor Street
London W1

© 1979 Martin Gilbert

This book was designed and produced by
George Rainbird Ltd
40 Park Street, London W1Y 4DE

ISBN 0 907486 27 4

Printed in Singapore

AUTHOR'S ACKNOWLEDGMENT
I am grateful to all those who have made this
book possible, including Gerry Moeran of Studio
Edmark, Oxford, for preparing much of the
photographic material, often from faded or
damaged originals; the copyright holders of all
material quoted in the text; and the owners and
copyright holders of the photographs, paintings
and documents listed on page 190.

FRONTISPIECE Churchill as a Harrow
schoolboy.

ENDPAPERS Woven cotton and artificial silk,
c. 1931.

 # Contents

1
Youth
1874-1900

Winston Churchill was born at Blenheim Palace on 30 November 1874. His family was a famous one. His father, Lord Randolph Churchill, became a Member of Parliament, a brilliant orator, and a Cabinet Minister. The Churchills were direct descendants of the first Duke of Marlborough, John Churchill, the hero of the Battle of Blenheim in 1704. All his life, Churchill was proud of his great ancestor, 'Duke John'. As a schoolboy, he learned by heart the description of Marlborough's victories carved in stone on the great column at Blenheim Palace. When Churchill was a boy, and a guest at Blenheim, he would study the tapestries which depicted those victories of nearly two hundred years before. Later, as an artist, he himself set up his easel at Blenheim, and painted the tapestries time and time again. In the 1930s he devoted nearly five years to writing a four-volume history of his ancestor's career.

Churchill's mother, Lady Randolph Churchill, was an American, with Red Indian blood in her veins; a beautiful woman, and a friend of many of the leading figures of British society. Among her friends were politicians, writers, and artists. From his father, Churchill acquired the traditions of the English aristocracy: self-confidence, ambition, and a desire to get to the root of the matter. From his mother came that pioneering spirit, that total lack of pretence, that hatred of snobbery, and that belief in the powers of one's own star and in the importance of one's personal abilities which had driven forward to a series of new frontiers the men and women who had built the United States.

FACING PAGE One of the tapestries at Blenheim Palace showing the victories of John Churchill, first Duke of Marlborough.

In his memoirs of his childhood, *My Early Life*, Churchill wrote in 1930: 'I was a child of the Victorian era, when the structure of our country seemed firmly set, when its position in trade and on the seas was unrivalled, and when the realization of the greatness of our Empire and of our duty to preserve it was ever growing stronger.'

7

Parents

Churchill spent most of his early childhood under the care of his nurse, and of a governess. As a result, he saw little of his mother. Later, he wrote of her: 'She shone for me like the Evening Star. I loved her dearly – but at a distance.'

Churchill saw equally little of his father, but was devoted to him nevertheless. 'We saw as children', he wrote, 'the passers-by take off their hats in the street and the workmen grin when they saw his big moustache. For years I had read every word he spoke and what the newspapers said about him.'

Churchill learned many of his father's speeches by heart and enjoyed going to the House of Commons to listen to the debates. At his father's house he met many of the leading politicians of the day.

ABOVE Churchill's mother.

BELOW A cartoon of Churchill's father (standing left), showing him with his colleagues in the Fourth Party, a wing of the Conservative Party, in 1880.

FACING PAGE Churchill's father painted by Edwin Long, 1888.

THE FOURTH PARTY.

Churchill's nurse,
Mrs Everest.

Schooldays

Churchill's closest companion during his childhood was his nurse, Mrs Everest. The names he gave her were 'Woom' and 'Woomany', and she was devoted to him. During his schooldays she took him to her sister's home on the Isle of Wight. 'It was to her', he later wrote, 'I poured out my many troubles.'

At the age of thirteen Churchill went, as a boarder, to Harrow School, where he remained for four and a half years. Although he did badly at Latin, he did well at English. Indeed, while he was still in the lowest form, he won a school prize for recitation. But he was unhappy at school, and later declared: 'I would far rather have been apprenticed as a bricklayer's mate, or run errands as a messenger boy, or helped my father to dress the front window of a grocer's shop. It would have been more real; it would have been more natural; it would have taught me more; and I should have done it much better!'

ABOVE The house on the Isle of Wight where Churchill spent some of his school holidays.

BELOW The 'Headmaster's' house, where Churchill spent eleven of his terms at Harrow.

Soldier

At the age of eighteen, Churchill entered the army as a cadet. Just over a year later, his father died, at the early age of forty-five. Churchill later wrote: 'a boy deprived of his father's care often develops, if he escapes the perils of youth, an independence and a vigour of thought which may restore in after life the heavy loss of early days'.

As a young soldier, Churchill first saw action on the north-west frontier of India. Then, at the age of twenty-three, he took part in the war in the Sudan, where he charged with the British cavalry at the Battle of Omdurman. Some of his closest friends were killed or wounded during the battle. When it was over, Churchill wrote a book about it called *The River War*.

FACING PAGE:

ABOVE LEFT The war in the Sudan, one of the maps from Churchill's own book about the campaign.

BELOW The telegram sent by Churchill's mother to his Aunt Leonie immediately after the Battle of Omdurman, announcing: 'Winston all right'.

ABOVE RIGHT The cover of Churchill's book, *The River War*, showing a British gunboat on the Nile and the Mahdi's tomb, damaged by shellfire.

BELOW Fancy dress at Sandhurst; Churchill is the clown in the back row.

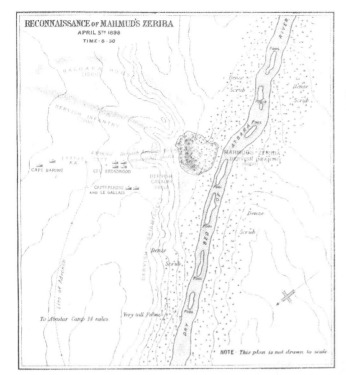

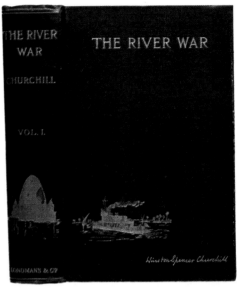

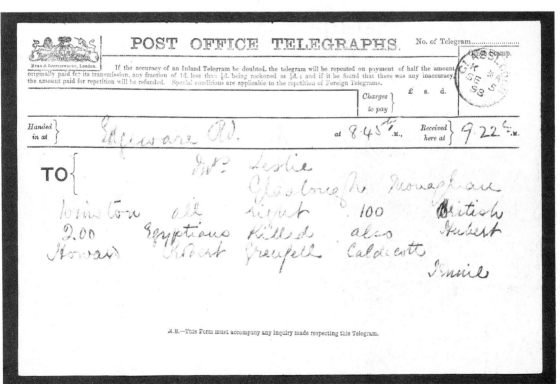

Prisoner-of-war

After the Battle of Omdurman, Churchill returned to England, left the army, and stood for Parliament. But he was defeated by a narrow margin. 'Everyone threw the blame on me', he wrote. 'I have noticed that they nearly always do.'

In 1899 Churchill sailed from England for South Africa, as a newspaper correspondent, to report on the Boer War. While travelling with the troops in an armoured train, he was taken prisoner by the Boers.

Imprisoned at Pretoria, in a prisoner-of-war camp, Churchill escaped. His escape made headline news.

FACING PAGE The armoured train in which Churchill was travelling when he was captured by the Boers; this book, in which he described his experiences, was published immediately on his return to England.

BELOW British prisoners-of-war taken to Pretoria, the Boer capital; Churchill is standing on the right.

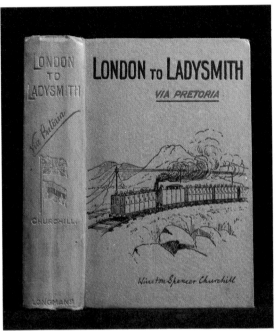

BELOW Churchill's escape from Pretoria was celebrated in England by popular artists, making him famous overnight.

FAMOUS ESCAPES

Winston Churchill's Escape from Pretoria.

The Hero

After his escape from the Boers, Churchill returned to Durban a hero, and at once gave up his status as a newspaper correspondent to rejoin the army.

When the war was over, he lectured about his escape, and about his other war experiences, to audiences throughout England and the United States. Now, well known, he stood once more for election to Parliament, as a Conservative.

ABOVE Churchill arrives at Durban after his escape from the prisoner-of-war camp in Pretoria and is given a triumphant welcome.

LEFT Back in the army.

FACING PAGE A poster announcing one of Churchill's lectures after his return to England.

PARK HALL, CARDIFF.

The Committee of the Cardiff Naturalists Society beg to announce that Mr.

Winston Churchill, M.P.

Will give his deeply interesting Lecture, entitled :

"THE WAR AS I SAW IT"

ON

THURSDAY EVENING, NOVEMBER 29th, 1900, at 8.

The Lecture will be illustrated by Lantern Slides from Photos.

Mr. J. J. NEALE (*President of the Cardiff Naturalists Society*), will preside.

Doors open at 7.30.   Lecture at 8.   Carriages at 9.45.

RESERVED SEATS—Balcony, Front Row, 7/6; [Other Seats in Balcony, 5/-; Area, 3/6; UNRESERVED SEATS, 2/-.

Plan of the Hall may be seen and Tickets obtained at Mr. WM. LEWIS's, Duke Street.

Even before he entered Parliament, Churchill was already known to the public as 'Winston'. This drawing by 'Spy' was published in *Vanity Fair* on 27 September 1900, during Churchill's election campaign in Oldham. Four days later the result was announced: Churchill was now a Member of Parliament.

2

Young Statesman
1900-1914

Churchill became a Member of Parliament in 1900, at the age of twenty-five. Although he was a member of the Conservative Party, he did not hesitate to criticize his own party and its leaders. Only three months after he had entered Parliament, he warned the House of Commons, in a sombre speech, that any future European war would not only ruin the states that were defeated, but would also exhaust the states that won.

Churchill led a busy life, not only in politics. During 1901, his first year in Parliament, he gave thirty public lectures, made nine speeches in the House of Commons, spent fourteen days hunting, and twelve afternoons playing polo. That same year, after reading a book about the living conditions of the poor in York, he denounced such conditions as 'terrible and shocking', and urged Parliament to play a more active part in improving working conditions. Three years later, in 1904, he joined the Liberal Party, and for the next six years, championed the rights of the poor and needy. At the same time, he established a reputation as a fine speaker, and as a man of almost unbounded energy. In 1908 a leading journalist wrote in an essay on Churchill: 'He is extraordinarily youthful even for his years. He has the curiosity and animation of a child – a child in fairyland, a child consumed with the thirst for life. He must know all, taste all, devour all. He is drunk with the wonder and fascination of living. A talk with him is as exhilarating as a gallop across country, so full is it of adventure, and of the high spirits and eagerness of youth. No matter what the subject, soldiering or science, religion or literature, he plunges into it with the joy of a boy taking a "header" in the sea. And to the insatiable curiosity and the enthusiasm of the boy he joins the frankness of the child. He has no reserves and no shams.'

Politics and Writing

As a bachelor, Churchill lived in London, active in politics, and writing several books. Before he was thirty years old he had published four books on his war experiences – in India, the Sudan and South Africa – a romantic novel, and a slim volume of collected speeches. He had also begun to write a biography of his father. Throughout these bachelor years, Churchill's mother encouraged him in his political career.

For some years Churchill was worried about the effect on his career of a slight speech defect, or lisp. In order to pronounce the letter 's' properly, he used to walk up and down with one of his girl friends, Muriel Wilson, practising again and again this sentence: 'The Spanish ships I cannot see, for they are not in sight.' Later he proposed to Miss Wilson, but she turned him down. In 1904 he met, briefly, at a dance, the nineteen-year-old Clementine Hozier, who was later to become his wife.

ABOVE Muriel Wilson, a drawing by John Sargent.

ABOVE Churchill during his first year in
Parliament. He became a Member of Parliament
two months before his twenty-sixth birthday.

FACING PAGE Churchill's mother, writing at her
desk in London. She was then editor of a
magazine called *Anglo-Saxon Review*.

RIGHT Clementine Hozier.

Young Liberal

In 1904, after only four years as a Conservative Member of Parliament Churchill became a Liberal. As a result of changing parties, he had to find a new Parliamentary constituency. His choice was North-West Manchester, a Conservative stronghold. Churchill won the seat at the General Election of 1906, the election at which the Liberal Party came to power.

Even as a young man, Churchill's character and success made him a focal point of comment. Indeed, as early as 1905, when he was still thirty, the first of many Churchill biographies was published. In it, the biographer wrote of Churchill: 'In every work to which he has put his hand he has excelled. He will ever be a leader, whether of a forlorn hope or of a great party. Already in the House of Commons he leads by a natural right which no man can dispute.'

Churchill at a garden party in his constituency, North-West Manchester, on 23 August 1907.

In the Government

FACING PAGE Churchill with Eddie Marsh, his Private Secretary, a photograph taken in Malta in 1907.

As Under-Secretary of State for the Colonies, Churchill came in contact with many of the leaders of the British Empire. He also met the future Indian leader, Gandhi, who came to see him on behalf of the Indians of South Africa. Gandhi later recalled with pleasure Churchill's helpful attitude.

While he was at the Colonial Office, Churchill was given a Private Secretary, Eddie Marsh. For the next twenty years, whenever Churchill held Government Office, Marsh would join him, helping him with his appointments and correspondence, keeping any unwelcome callers at bay, and accompanying Churchill on most of his official work.

Churchill (standing far left) at the Imperial Conference held in London on 8 May 1907; in front of him is the Chancellor of the Exchequer, H. H. Asquith, later Prime Minister; his friend Lloyd George is seated on the far right.

ABOVE Churchill and his companions ford the River Asua.

BELOW Churchill on safari in East Africa, with a Burchell's White Rhinoceros.

Journey through Africa

In the summer of 1906 Churchill went by ship to East Africa. Then he travelled by train inland to Uganda, combining official work with hunting and shooting, and spending twenty days on safari with his uncle by marriage, Colonel Gordon Wilson – who took the photographs – and his Private Secretary, Eddie Marsh.

While he was travelling, Churchill wrote regular accounts of what he saw for a magazine. On his return to England, they were published in a book called *My African Journey*, in which he wrote of how, 'if the landscape recalls to the pensive traveller the peaceful beauty of gentler climes at home, let him remember that it nurses with blithe fecundity poisonous reptiles, and pest-spreading insects, and terrible beasts of prey'.

FACING PAGE Churchill's book written on his return from East Africa, describing his adventures.

MY AFRICAN JOURNEY

BY THE RT. HON.
WINSTON SPENCER CHURCHILL
M.P.

Return from Africa

Churchill returned from East Africa along the full length of the River Nile, northwards from Lake Victoria. His journey took him to Omdurman, where nine years earlier he had taken part in the cavalry charge that helped to defeat the Dervish army. Churchill was much impressed by the development of Khartoum since he had last seen it. Now, he wrote, it was 'a smiling city sitting like a queen throned at the confluence of the Niles, the heart and centre of a far-reaching and formidable authority'.

But Churchill's return was also a time of personal sadness, for, as he recalled: 'As our steamer approached the landing-stage I learned that my English servant, George Scrivings, had been taken suddenly ill, and found him in a condition of prostration with a strange blue colour under his skin. Good doctors were summoned. The hospital of Khartoum, with all its resources, was at hand. There appeared no reason to apprehend a fatal termination. But he had been seized by a violent internal inflammation, the result of eating some poisonous thing which we apparently had escaped, and died early next morning after fifteen hours' illness.'

Churchill's account continued: 'Too soon, indeed, had I ventured to rejoice. Africa

always claims its forfeits; and so the four white men who had started together from Mombasa returned but three to Cairo. . . . The day after the Battle of Omdurman it had fallen to my lot to bury those soldiers of the 21st Lancers, who had died of their wounds during the night. Now after nine years, in very different circumstances, from the other end of Africa, I had come back to this grim place where so much blood has been shed, and again I found myself standing at an open grave, while the yellow glare of the departed sun still lingered over the desert, and the sound of funeral volleys broke its silence.'

ABOVE George Scrivings, a photograph taken four days before his death.

FACING PAGE Churchill in the Governor's Palace at Khartoum, showing the marks of the British bombardment of 1898; Eddie Marsh is seated on the right.

Engagement and Marriage

In April 1908 Churchill entered the Cabinet, as President of the Board of Trade. He was only thirty-three years old. On the weekend of his appointment, he spent the Sunday at his mother's house north of London. There he again met Clementine Hozier. She was now twenty-three years old and their friendship began. Four months later they were engaged to be married. In September 1908 as Churchill himself wrote: 'I married and lived happily ever afterwards.'

ABOVE An engagement portrait published in a German magazine.

ABOVE The only known photograph of Churchill (front row) and Clementine Hozier (second row) showing them together during their engagement. Also in the photograph are his brother Jack, his aunt Lady Sarah Wilson, and her husband Colonel Gordon Wilson, his brother's fiancée Lady Gwendeline Churchill, his cousin the 9th Duke of Marlborough and several close friends, including Valentine Fleming, father of Ian and Peter Fleming. The photograph was taken at a meeting of The Queen's Own Oxfordshire Hussars in Blenheim Park, when the King of Portugal was the guest of the Regiment.

Radical Politics

In politics, Churchill was emerging as a leader
of the radical wing of the Liberal Party. He
wanted the state to play a direct part in re-
lieving the distress of the working class.
Working closely in the Cabinet with his colleague, David Lloyd George, Churchill de-
vised measures to end sweated labour, to
ensure a fair basic minimum wage for the low
paid, to provide the unemployed with insur-
ance, and to set up Labour Exchanges where
the unemployed could find work. In his pamphlet *The People's Rights*, published in 1909, he
advocated 'a smashing blow' to end the veto
powers of the House of Lords to hold up these
reforms.

BELOW Churchill campaigning in his constituency
in April 1908, when he had to seek re-election
upon his appointment as President of the Board
of Trade. He was defeated, but re-elected shortly
afterwards for Dundee.

RIGHT Churchill's pamphlet *The People's Rights*.

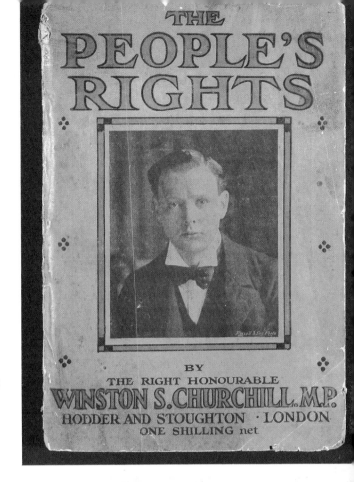

THE
PEOPLE'S
RIGHTS

BY
THE RIGHT HONOURABLE
WINSTON S. CHURCHILL, M.P.
HODDER AND STOUGHTON · LONDON
ONE SHILLING net

BELOW In 1910 Churchill became Home Secretary; here he is seen attending army manoeuvres on Salisbury Plain; next to him is Sir John French, who was later to command the British Expeditionary Force in France.

Labour Exchanges and Prison Reform

In 1909 and 1910, as President of the Board of Trade, Churchill had set up the first Labour Exchanges in which the unemployed received help from the Government in finding work.

In February 1910, when he was still only thirty-five, Churchill became Home Secretary. It was a troubled time, with strikes and riots in South Wales and Lancashire. But it was also a time of constructive work for Churchill. He had never forgotten the humiliation of being a prisoner in South Africa, and was determined to make life less hard for the men in Britain's prisons. So successful was he in improving prison conditions, in reducing the number of prisoners between the ages of sixteen and twenty-one, in shortening the amount of time spent in solitary confinement, in pro-

viding lectures and concerts inside the prisons, and in setting up a special after-care association to help convicts after they had served their sentence, that this led the dramatist and prison reformer, John Galsworthy, to write, in a letter to Churchill's aunt: 'I have always admired his pluck and his capacity. I now perceive him to have a heart and to be very warm.'

FACING PAGE Churchill and his wife opening one of the first Labour Exchanges in London on 1 February 1910.

BELOW On 30 June 1910 Churchill accompanied Mrs Lloyd George, Lloyd George and his secretary, on the way to Parliament for Lloyd George's controversial 'People's' Budget.

First Lord of the Admiralty

In October 1911 Churchill became First Lord of the Admiralty. For nearly three years he worked to prepare the Royal Navy for a possible war with Germany. Ships' fuel was changed from coal to oil. Faster, better armed ships were built. Mobilization plans were perfected. At naval manoeuvres, the war capacity of the fleet was tested. Conditions in the daily life of the sailors were improved. Promotion from the lower decks to officer rank was made easier.

In May 1912 Churchill steamed to the Mediterranean on board the Admiralty yacht *Enchantress*. With him on board was the Prime Minister, Asquith, and Asquith's daughter Violet. They visited Italy and Malta, combining discussions of naval strategy with sightseeing and relaxation.

Churchill became such a determined champion of the Navy that on one occasion his friend Lloyd George told him: 'You have become a water creature. You think we all live in the sea, and all your thoughts are devoted to sea life, fishes and other aquatic creatures. You forget that most of us live on land.'

LEFT Churchill on board the Admiralty yacht, *Enchantress*, in the Firth of Forth.

FACING PAGE ABOVE: Admiral of the Fleet Prince Louis of Battenberg, Asquith and Churchill during the Mediterranean cruise of 1912.

FACING PAGE BELOW Clementine Churchill.

Air Pioneer

In 1912 Churchill set up a special Royal Naval Air Service whose aeroplanes and seaplanes were to defend Britain's harbours and oil tanks. He also established an Air Department at the Admiralty, so that the problems of naval aviation could, as he wrote, be 'continuously gripped and studied'.

For two years, Churchill encouraged the development of flying, and set aside funds from his Admiralty budget to encourage the new science. In a series of instructions, he stressed the need for 'a standard wireless to be quickly and easily fitted', for 'care and attention' to be paid to the problem of comfortable seating for pilot and observer, for further research into the use of aerial torpedoes, and for the establishment of 'certain well-marked flying routes along which at known intervals good landing places will be available'.

Churchill argued that it was the 'falsest economy' to have cheap engine controls. And he insisted that the conditions of service for pilots should be such as 'to make aviation for war purposes the most honourable, as it is the most dangerous profession a young Englishman can adopt'.

In 1913, while he was still First Lord of the Admiralty, Churchill decided to learn to fly. At that time, thirty-two was considered the top age to take up flying. Churchill was thirty-eight. But he relished the challenge of flight, and whenever he could spare the time from his Cabinet duties, he would drive to the naval air station at Eastchurch, and take to the air.

FACING PAGE A *Punch* cartoon of 25 March 1914.

BELOW This photograph was taken on 23 February 1914 when Churchill himself piloted this seaplane as part of his flying instruction.

NEPTUNE'S ALLY.

(The FIRST LORD OF THE ADMIRALTY calls in a new element to redress the balance of the old.)

Accident in the Air

Churchill's first flying instructor was Captain Gilbert Wildman Lushington. In a letter to his fiancée, Airlie Hynes, Lushington wrote in November 1913: 'I started Winston off in his instruction about 12.15 and he got so bitten with it, I could hardly get him out of the machine.'

Three days later, Lushington, while flying solo, crashed while coming in to land, and was killed. After the funeral, his fiancée wrote to Churchill: 'He was so pleased at having given you your first instruction, and his last letters were all about it and he was so happy.'

Churchill's friends now urged him to give up flying. But he continued to practise, and within six months of his first flight he was only a few mornings away from getting his pilot's certificate. His wife was worried, however, by the dangers, and in June 1914 she urged him to give up flying. As she was expecting their third child, Churchill agreed. He had flown as a co-pilot on nearly 140 separate occasions.

BELOW Churchill's flying instructor, Gilbert Wildman Lushington, a postcard published in the 'Flying at Hendon Series' while Lushington was still a Lieutenant.

FACING PAGE ABOVE A postcard of Lushington's funeral; the caption reads: 'Funeral of Captain Wildman Lushington RMA, Mr Churchill's Air Pilot.'

FACING PAGE BELOW Churchill piloting a seaplane over Portsmouth Harbour.

LIEUT W. LUSHINGTON.

"FLYING AT HENDON SERIES"

Funeral of Captain Wildman-Lushington R.M.A.
Mr Churchill's Air Pilot   Dec. 1913

ABOVE Shaking hands with the Kaiser at German
army manoeuvres in September 1909.

FACING PAGE BELOW Churchill inspecting British
naval installations in the summer of 1914; with
him is Field-Marshal Sir John French.

Eve of War, 1914

In the five years leading up to the First World War, Churchill had spent many hours at military manoeuvres, not only in Britain, but in France and Germany. In 1906 he had been the guest of the Kaiser at German manoeuvres. As a result of what he saw of the German army at war-practice he told one of his aunts: 'I am very thankful there is a sea between that army and Britain.'

In the summer of 1914, as part of his naval preparations, Churchill authorized a test mobilization of the Fleet. While the Fleet was assembled in the English Channel, the Sarajevo assassination threatened war in Europe. Churchill ordered the warships not to disperse, and as the crisis deepened, he sent the First Fleet, secretly, through the Straits of Dover, to its war station in the North Sea.

Nine months later, when Churchill's career was in ruins, Lord Kitchener told him: 'Well, there is one thing at any rate they cannot take from you. The Fleet was ready.'

RIGHT The front cover of the *Tatler* magazine of 12 August 1914, eight days after the outbreak of the First World War.

BRAVO WINSTON!

The Rapid Naval Mobilisation and Purchase of the Two Foreign Dreadnoughts Spoke Volumes for your Work and Wisdom.

MR. WINSTON CHURCHILL, FIRST LORD OF THE ADMIRALTY
AND (INSET) HIS CHARMING AND BEAUTIFUL WIFE

FIELD·MARSHAL·SIR·JOHN·FRENCH

KING·GEORGE·V

THE·RIGHT·HON·
D·LLOYD·GEORGE

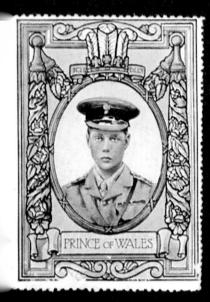

PRINCE·OF·WALES

RT·HON·WINSTON·CHURCHILL

SIR·EDWARD·GREY

EMPEROR·OF·JAPAN

GENERAL·FOCH

KING·OF·MONTENEGRO

3

The First World War 1914-1918

For Churchill, the start of the First World War was a time of great power and responsibility. As First Lord of the Admiralty, he was in charge of the Royal Navy, whose ships and sailors had not only to protect Britain from invasion, but also to transport the British Expeditionary Force to France.

Churchill's work extended beyond the Admiralty. As a member of the Government's inner War Council, his views were sought, and his voice was heard, over every aspect of war policy. On many occasions, his Cabinet colleagues turned to him for a balanced judgment.

In a few months, however, all this had changed. A force of British naval troops, which Churchill sent to the Belgian city of Antwerp in October 1914, was unable to prevent the city's capture by a far larger German force. Churchill's own arrival at Antwerp, to help supervise the city's defence, became the subject of much derisive comment. Then, in May 1915, the Navy tried to defeat Germany's ally, Turkey, by driving the Turks from the Dardanelles. But even the most powerful naval guns, and the most modern battleships were unable to dislodge the Turks from their cliff top defences. When an attack by British battleships was halted by a Turkish minefield, Churchill wanted to try again. But a political crisis in England led to his removal from the Admiralty.

For six months Churchill remained in the Cabinet, but without any real power to influence the Government's war policy. In an attempt to put his distress out of his mind, he began a new hobby, painting. Then he rejoined the Army, and went to France.

FACING PAGE Nine Allied leaders: cigarette cards issued shortly after the outbreak of war in 1914.

In July 1917 the new Prime Minister, Lloyd George, brought Churchill back into the Government as Minister of Munitions. For more than a year, he was in charge of the production of tanks, aeroplanes, guns and shells.

First Months of War

On the outbreak of war in 1914, the cartoonists celebrated Churchill's reputation for energetic action. His friend and Cabinet colleague, Lloyd George, later recalled how, on the night war was declared: 'Winston dashed into the room, radiant, his face bright, his manner keen, one word pouring out on another how he was going to send telegrams to the Mediterranean, the North Sea, and God knows where. You could see he was really a happy man.'

Yet the early months of the war saddened Churchill, as they saddened so many people. His nephew Norman was killed in action in October 1914. Within a month, his uncle by marriage, Gordon Wilson, had also been killed. His brother Jack was serving in France. Many of his best friends had gone to the front; two of them had already been killed, on the same day as his uncle. There was, however, one moment of joy, the birth of a second daughter, Sarah, in the third month of the war.

A Churchill family portrait at the end of 1914, showing Churchill, his daughter Diana, Clementine Churchill with the newly born Sarah, his son Randolph, his mother Lady Randolph Churchill, Lady Gwendeline Churchill with her two sons Peregrine and John-George (standing) and Churchill's brother Jack, then serving on the Western Front.

One of the many cartoons of Churchill published
on the first day of the war, 4 August 1914; this
one, by Poy, was called 'Full Steam Ahead'.

47

Royal Naval units reach Antwerp at the end of
September 1914.

The Siege of Antwerp

Within two weeks of the outbreak of war, Churchill had set up a new military unit, the Royal Naval Division, under Admiralty control. Many of Churchill's friends asked him if they could join, and many young men, including the poet Rupert Brooke, were delighted to have a chance of going into action.

Early in September 1914 the Belgian Government appealed to Britain to send military help to the defence of Antwerp. Churchill sent the Royal Marines, and then, as reinforcements, the newly formed Naval Division. Although many of these troops were poorly equipped, they were the only men that could be spared from the battles then raging in France.

As the Germans advanced on Antwerp, Churchill hurriedly left London, hoping to persuade the Belgians not to surrender. The extra British troops arrived. But the strength of the German forces, and the power of the German guns, was overwhelming. Churchill returned to London. The British troops retreated, many of them being taken prisoner, and Antwerp surrendered.

On his return to London, Churchill found himself at the centre of a storm of criticism. One newspaper told its readers that Churchill had yet to learn 'that he is not, as a matter of fact, a Napoleon, but a Minister of the Crown, with no time either to organize, or to lead armies in the field'. But Churchill was certain that the war could only be won if initiatives were taken and risks were run. Nor did he underrate, or shun, the consequences of failure.

German soldiers pose in front of their booty in Antwerp, November 1914; this photograph and its caption were published in London in 1914 by *The Times History of the War* weekly magazine.

The Dardanelles

It was with the failure of the naval attack at the Dardanelles that Churchill's fortunes fell to their lowest ebb. The Secretary of State for War, Lord Kitchener, had been reluctant to send troops to the Dardanelles. Churchill tried to defeat the Turks by ships alone. The ships failed. A political crisis followed in London, and Churchill was forced to leave the Admiralty.

Meanwhile, Kitchener agreed to send troops. But they arrived only after the naval attack had foundered on a Turkish minefield. The troops then landed, on the Gallipoli peninsula overlooking the Dardanelles. But after nearly nine months of bloodshed, they too failed to dislodge the Turks, and had to be withdrawn. For the rest of his life, on election platforms and at public meetings, Churchill was to be taunted with the cry: 'What about the Dardanelles?'

ABOVE Field-Marshal Earl Kitchener of Khartoum, Secretary of State for War at the time of the Gallipoli landings, detail of a painting by H. von Herkoner, 1890.

FACING PAGE ABOVE The Gallipoli landings – the scene at V-Beach; the ship in the background is the *River Clyde*, which, filled with troops, was deliberately beached at the beginning of the landings on 25 April 1915.

FACING PAGE BELOW British troops on the Gallipoli Peninsula.

ABOVE Asquith at the time of the formation of his Coalition Government in May 1915.

Cast down

With the initial failure of the sea and land attacks at the Dardanelles, the Conservative opposition demanded a place in the Government. The Prime Minister, Asquith, gave in to this demand. As part of the Conservative conditions for joining the new Government, Churchill had to leave the Admiralty. He remained in the Cabinet, but without any means to influence policy.

This was a bitter time for Churchill. He was convinced that a further naval and land attack at Gallipoli could defeat the Turks, and thus shorten the war. But a second attack, in August 1915, was again a failure. In London, Churchill was powerless. He even thought of going out to Gallipoli himself. Finally, in November 1915, he resigned from the Cabinet, and decided to go to France, to the Western Front, as a soldier.

Many people were sad to see Churchill go. Indeed, just before he left, Asquith's daughter Violet wrote to him: 'Come back to us very soon, and remember that England trusts and needs you.' And to the House of Commons, Churchill declared: 'There is no reason to be discouraged about the progress of the war. We are passing through a bad time now, and it will probably be worse before it is better. But that it will be better, if only we endure and persevere, I have no doubt whatever.'

FACING PAGE BELOW Churchill on the Western
Front, visiting French forces in dugouts near the
Channel coast; he has already discovered the
value of the French helmet as opposed to the
British tin hat.

ABOVE A painting of Churchill in 1916 by Sir John
Lavery.

At the Front

Churchill's first month on the Western Front was spent in training with the Grenadier Guards. He also visited units of the French army, and was much impressed by the superiority of their steel helmets to the tin hats of the British tommy. In January 1916 he took command of a Scottish battalion which had suffered greatly in the battles of 1915. For nearly four weeks he trained them behind the lines, and then, for three months, he commanded them in the front line. On several occasions he was nearly killed by shellfire. 'In war', he reflected, 'chance casts aside all veils and disguises, and presents herself nakedly from moment to moment. . . . You may walk to the right or to the left of a particular tree, and it makes the difference whether you rise to command an Army Corps, or are sent home crippled and paralysed for life.'

BELOW Lieutenant-Colonel Churchill with his second-in-command, Major Sir Archibald Sinclair – later to become leader of the Liberal Party.

BELOW The 6th Battalion, Royal Scots Fusiliers, a
photograph taken during Churchill's command.

In the Trenches

Churchill's battalion was billeted in the Belgian village of Ploegsteert, known to the British by the colloquial name, 'Plugstreet'. The farms in which the soldiers lived, the dug-outs, and the village itself, were under continual German rifle and shell fire. As his officers prepared to take up their front-line duties, Churchill told them: 'Don't be careless about yourselves – on the other hand not too careful. Keep a special pair of boots to sleep in and only get them muddy in a real emergency. Use alcohol in moderation but don't have a great parade of bottles in your dug-outs. Live well but do not flaunt it. Laugh a little, and teach your men to laugh – great good humour under fire – war is a game that is played with a smile. If you can't smile grin. If you can't grin keep out of the way till you can.'

Churchill commanded his battalion on the Western Front for a hundred days. During that time fifteen of his men were killed and more than a hundred wounded. Churchill was vigilant in caring for his men, and in making sure that they were well protected against shell fire. He also found time to practise his new hobby, painting. One of the young officers of the battalion later recalled how: 'Winston started painting the second or third time he went up to the farm. Each time we were in the line he spent some time on his paintings. Gradually, too, the courtyard became more pitted with shell-holes. As his painting came nearer to completion, he became morose, angry, and exceedingly difficult to talk to. After five or six days in this mood, he suddenly appeared cheerful and delighted, like a small

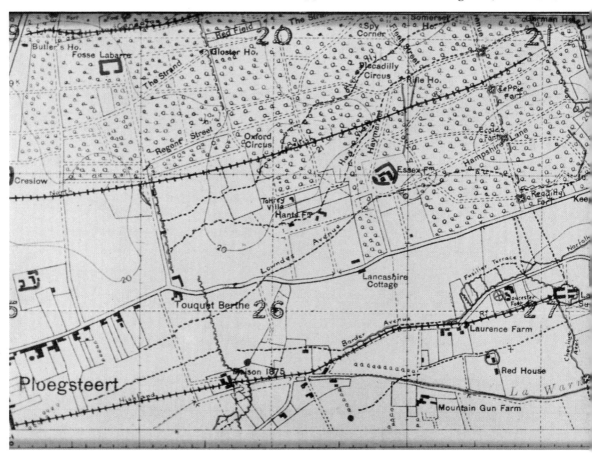

boy at school. I asked him what had happened, and he said, "I have been worried because I couldn't get the shell-hole right in the painting. However I did it, it looked like a mountain, but yesterday I discovered that if I put a little bit of white in it, it looked like a hole after all." '

Churchill's front-line experiences in 1916 taught him a great deal about the dangers, and horrors, of trench warfare. His men recalled how he would often go into no-man's-land on night patrol, risking his life in order to ensure that the battalion's defences were secure.

On his return to London Churchill told the House of Commons: 'the trench population lives almost continuously under the fire of the enemy. It returns again and again, after being wounded twice and sometimes three times, to the front and to the trenches, and it is continually subject, without respite, to the hardest of tests that men have ever been called upon to bear.'

A trench map of Churchill's battalion front. The British trenches are marked in green, the German trenches in red. Churchill's headquarters were at Laurence Farm and his forward observation post at Burnt Out Farm. The area under Churchill's direct responsibility was between the edge of the wood and the Warnave brook. On one occasion, while walking past the Convent, Churchill was nearly killed by German shell fire.

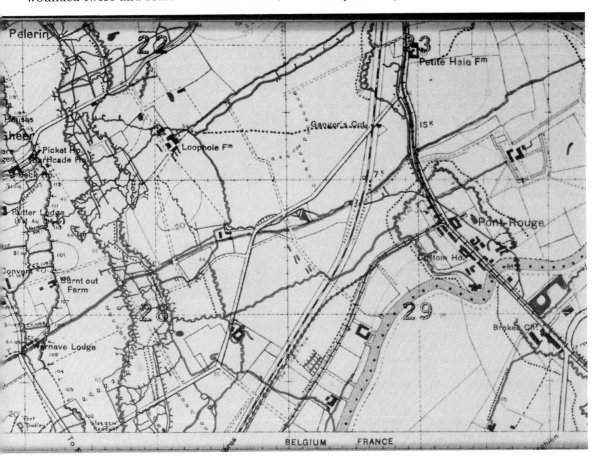

A portrait of Churchill
painted in 1915 by
Ernest Townsend.

Mementos of the First World War: clockwise
from left: A book written by Andrew Dewar Gibb,
who served with Churchill in the trenches: a
photograph of Churchill with members of his
regiment, the 6th Royal Scots Fusiliers: a letter
from the front from Churchill to Venetia
Montagu: one of Churchill's Admiralty directives.

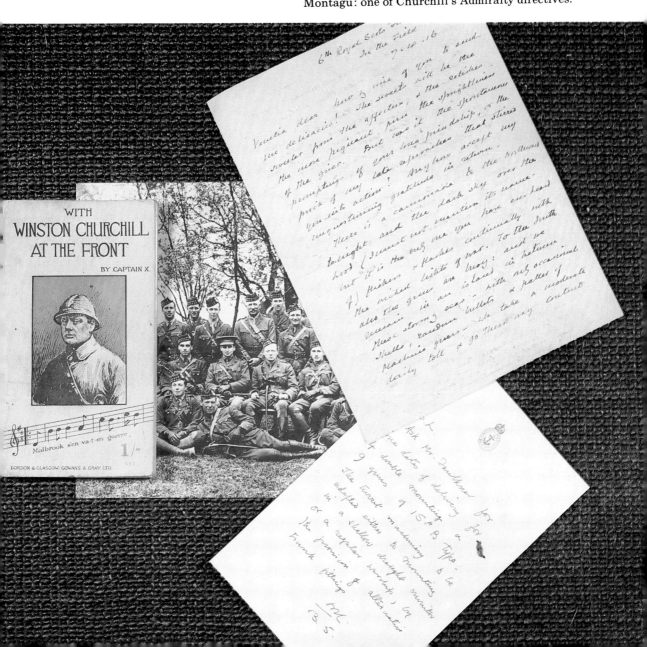

Minister of Munitions

After his return from the trenches, Churchill spent a year as a backbench Member of Parliament. In December 1916 his friend Lloyd George became Prime Minister, and seven months later he brought Churchill into the Government, as Minister of Munitions. Churchill now set to work on a new task, to make the guns, shells, tanks and aeroplanes on which victory would depend. He worked both in London, and in France, where a château not far from the front line served as his headquarters.

While he was working at his French château, Churchill made several visits to the front line. Of one of these, in September 1917, Eddie Marsh, who travelled with him, wrote: 'Winston was attracted by the sight of shells bursting in the distance – irresistible! Out we got, put on our steel helmets, hung our gas-masks round our necks, and walked for half-an-hour towards the firing, there was a great noise, shells whistling over our heads, and some fine bursts in the distance – but we seemed to get no nearer, and the firing died down, so we went back after another hour's delay.' Marsh added: 'Winston's disregard of time, when there's anything he wants to do, is sublime – he firmly believes that it waits for him.'

ABOVE Clemenceau, the French Prime Minister, whom Churchill often saw in Paris during the final year of the war.

BELOW The château Verchocq, Churchill's headquarters in France while he was Minister of Munitions.

ABOVE The avenue of trees, likened by Churchill
to the aisle of a cathedral, in the grounds of the
château Verchocq.

Off duty

Whenever he could spare a weekend away
from London or France, Churchill would take
his work to Lullenden Manor, a house which
he had bought in Sussex in the spring of 1917,
and which was his and his family's retreat for
the rest of the war. There he painted, as well as
worked; and played with his son Randolph,
and his daughters Diana and Sarah.

One of Churchill's favourite games was the
Bear Game. Randolph, who was six years old
when his father bought Lullenden, later recalled how: 'Father was the Bear. We had to
turn our backs and close our eyes and he would
climb a tree. All us children – six or seven perhaps – had then to go and look for Bear. We
were very much afraid but would advance
courageously on a tree and say: "Bear! Bear!
Bear!" And then run away. Suddenly he would
drop from a tree and we would scatter in
various directions. He would pursue us and
the one he caught would be the loser.'

ABOVE Diana Churchill walking in Whitehall
with her nurse. In the perambulator is Randolph
Churchill. Photograph taken in 1914.

BELOW Diana, Randolph, and their cousin
John-George Spencer Churchill dressed for a
wedding in 1915.

The German Breakthrough

In March 1918 the Germans broke through the trench lines on the Western Front. For more than a month it looked as if the British and French might be defeated. Churchill's ability to produce the urgently needed munitions of war became a central feature of the war effort.

Churchill himself always regarded the British people as the true source of Britain's strength, telling the House of Commons in April 1918: 'No demand is too novel or too sudden to be met. No need is too unexpected to be supplied. No strain is too prolonged for the patience of our people. No suffering nor peril daunts their hearts. Instead of quarrelling, giving way as we do from time to time to moods of pessimism and of irritation, we ought to be thankful that if such trials and dangers were destined for our country we are here to share them, and to see them slowly and surely overcome.'

BELOW AND FACING PAGE Churchill visiting munitions factories, while Minister of Munitions; these two photographs were taken in Glasgow in October 1918.

GENERAL OFFICES.

65

Links with the United States

As Minister of Munitions, Churchill developed close links with the United States, and worked to draw in the Americans as much as possible to the war effort. On 4 July 1918, American Independence day, he told a meeting of the Anglo-Saxon Fellowship, at their Independence day dinner: 'When I have seen, during the past few weeks, the splendour of American manhood striding forward on all the roads of France and Flanders, I have experienced emotions which words cannot describe.'

Churchill and his wife at the Stamford Bridge baseball match on 4 July 1918; Churchill is wearing a Stars and Stripes streamer in his button hole.

Churchill inspecting British troops in Cologne,
August 1919.

The Coming of Victory

During the final months of the First World War, Churchill went several times to France on munitions business. Whenever he could, he flew. Fifty years later his pilot, Lieutenant Hall, recalled one such journey: 'It was dusk when we landed and his first remark was about the sunset we had just seen. At the aerodrome we found a group of young airmen, some little more than boys, waiting to take off on a night bombing raid. The engines of their machines were warming up and Mr Churchill strolled over for a chat. Later, as we moved away, he asked if I thought they looked depressed, as all were subdued and silent, and he then said – "You know, the people at home have no idea what these lads are going through".'

FACING PAGE In Paris after the Allied victory, Lloyd George entertains the three munitions' 'supremos', Louis Loucheur, the French Minister of Munitions, Churchill and Bernard Baruch, of the United States War Industries Board.

BELOW Lieutenant Gilbert Hall, Churchill's pilot, and the aeroplane in which he used to fly to France.

Minister of War

With the war ended, Churchill was put in charge of the massive and complex task of demobilization. As Secretary of State for War, he organized the return of millions of troops from Europe and the Middle East. At the same time, he had to keep in being an army large enough to maintain a British presence on the Rhine, in Turkey, and throughout the Middle East.

In October 1919 Churchill gave evidence to a Royal Commission which was enquiring into the invention of the tank. In its report the Commission stated 'that it was primarily due to the receptivity, courage and driving force of the Rt. Hon. Winston Spencer Churchill that the general idea of the use of such an instrument of warfare as the Tank was converted into practical shape'.

BELOW Churchill and the United States Ambassador (in civilian clothes) with the Prince of Wales and General Pershing, Commander of the United States Expeditionary Force, a photograph taken during a military review in July 1919.

FACING PAGE ABOVE Churchill begins his inspection of the British Army on the Rhine, August 1919.

FACING PAGE BELOW Churchill giving evidence at Lincoln's Inn, in October 1919, to the Royal Commission which enquired into the invention of the tank.

4

The Twenties

Churchill was forty-four years old when the First World War ended. He had been a Member of Parliament for nearly twenty years, and had held five different Cabinet posts. In the war itself, despite the criticisms of the Dardanelles, he had been noted for his abilities to work hard, and to inspire others to work hard.

The 1920s saw Churchill's career continue on its upward, if at times troubled, path. In Lloyd George's peacetime Government he was first Secretary of State for War, and then Secretary of State for the Colonies. In 1922 his daughter Mary was born.

Defeated at the polls in the General Election of October 1922, Churchill was out of Parliament for two years, but fought his way back. In 1924 he was elected to Parliament again, left the Liberal Party, and became Chancellor of the Exchequer in Stanley Baldwin's Conservative Government.

Henceforth, Churchill was a Conservative. But as Chancellor of the Exchequer, he continued to act with all his noted independence of mind. After the General Strike of 1926, he tried to secure a compromise settlement to the coal strike, which would give the miners a fair wage. As Chancellor of the Exchequer, he presented five budgets. He introduced a bold scheme of contributory pensions, including widows' pensions; and he raised death duties. He tried to legislate against tax evasion by private companies but Conservative pressure forced him to moderate his plan drastically. He paid much attention to lessening the tax burden on small incomes. Conservatives disliked his liberalist tendencies; while the Liberal leader Asquith noted with approval: 'He is a Chimborazo or Everest among the sand-hills of the Baldwin Cabinet.'

Colonial Secretary

At the beginning of 1921, Churchill was appointed Secretary of State for the Colonies, with special responsibilities towards the Middle East. He at once set up a Middle East Department at the Colonial Office, and brought in several experts on Arab affairs to help him, including Colonel T. E. Lawrence – better known as 'Lawrence of Arabia'. The main work concerned the territories taken from Turkey at the end of the First World War: Palestine, Transjordan and Iraq.

After two months of discussion with his advisers, Churchill set off for Cairo, where he summoned a Conference of all the senior British officials in the Middle East. Their aim was to work out a system of British control in the new areas, which would cost the British taxpayer as little as possible, and would lead to eventual independence for several Arab states.

During the Conference in Cairo, Lawrence of Arabia wrote to his brother, telling him of how 'we are a very happy family: agreed upon everything important; and the trifles are laughed at'. After eight days, the Conference took a break, and Churchill and his wife went for a camel ride at the Pyramids. During the ride, one newspaper reported, Churchill 'was thrown from his mount and grazed his hand badly, but insisted on continuing'.

BELOW The Cairo Conference, March 1921; on Churchill's right is Sir Herbert Samuel, the first British High Commissioner to Palestine, and on his left Sir Percy Cox, the High Commissioner in Iraq; T. E. Lawrence – 'Lawrence of Arabia' – is in civilian clothes behind Sir Percy Cox; Sir Archibald Sinclair is in the top row with a bow tie; in the foreground a Somali sergeant guards some lion cubs on their way from the Somaliland to the London Zoo.

FACING PAGE Clementine Churchill, Churchill, Gertrude Bell and T. E. Lawrence in front of the Sphinx.

FIDDLING WHILE ROME BURNS.

IMAGINE BEING CAUGHT LIKE THAT!

Cairo and Jerusalem

During the break in the Cairo conference, Churchill set up his easel at the Pyramids. On his return from one painting expedition his car was in a collision with another car but, as a local newspaper reported, Churchill himself was 'far more concerned about the safety of his painting than about himself'. The wife of one of the British officials at the conference later recalled how Churchill 'was always telling people not to give up their painting'.

From Cairo, Churchill travelled by train to Jerusalem, where he had several long meetings with the Emir Abdullah, whom Britain had decided to make ruler of Transjordan.

While he was in Palestine, Churchill visited the Jewish town of Tel Aviv, and one of the Jewish agricultural colonies. On his return to London he told the House of Commons how 'from the most inhospitable soil, surrounded on every side by barrenness and the most miserable form of cultivation, I was driven into a fertile and thriving country estate, where the scanty soil gave place to good crops and good cultivation, and then to vineyards and finally to the most beautiful luxurious orange groves, all created in twenty or thirty years by the exertions of the Jewish community who live there.'

FACING PAGE In March 1921 Bonar Law, the Lord Privy Seal, resigned his office. Churchill's chances for promotion in the ensuing Cabinet reshuffle were perhaps hampered by his absence in Egypt. This *Daily Mail* cartoon by Poy illustrates the incident.

BELOW The Emir Abdullah, Sir Herbert Samuel and Churchill; the Emir had just been appointed by Churchill as ruler of Transjordan.

Polo

From his early twenties until his fiftieth birthday, Churchill enjoyed playing polo, even though, as a result of having dislocated his shoulder as a young man, he had always to play with his right arm strapped to his chest. Even after he had given up playing polo, Churchill continued to ride horses for pleasure – until after his eightieth birthday.

RIGHT Churchill at the Roehampton Polo Ground in 1921.

BELOW With the Prince of Wales.

FACING PAGE Waiting to play.

A Year of Sorrow

Despite the absorbing work, and the pleasures of polo, 1921 was a sad year for Churchill. In June his mother died, as a result of falling down stairs. She was only sixty-seven years old. On hearing of her death, the Prime Minister, David Lloyd George, wrote to Churchill: 'I know how devoted she was to you, and you to her, and your grief must be profound'.

In August, a greater blow fell upon the Churchills, the death of their youngest daughter, Marigold. Deep in sorrow, Churchill went to stay with friends in Scotland, writing to his wife at the end of his first day away: 'I went out and painted a beautiful view in the afternoon light, with crimson and golden hills in the background. I hope to make it much better tomorrow.' And he added: 'Another twenty years will bring me to the end of my allotted span, even if I have so long. The reflections of middle age are mellow. I will take what comes.'

MINISTER BEREAVED

Mrs. Winston Churchill and her youngest child, Marigold Frances, who died last night at Overblow, South Cliff-parade, Broadstairs. The little one was three years old and was taken suddenly ill a week ago. Mr. Churchill, who had cancelled all public engagements, was present when the child passed away.

ABOVE Clementine Churchill with Marigold.

FACING PAGE *The World Crisis,* Churchill's six-volume history of the First World War. This set was presented by Churchill to his aunt, Lady Sarah Wilson.

During 1921 Churchill devoted much of his time to writing a volume of his war memoirs. He saw the book as an opportunity to vindicate his direction of naval affairs as First Lord of the Admiralty from 1911 to 1915, and especially his part in the controversial Dardanelles campaign. He sought documents from a wide range of sources both public and private, and enlisted the aid of experts and friends. On 29 December 1921 Churchill wrote to his wife that Lloyd George, Prime Minister during the last two years of the war, was helping with the book, and had 'praised the style' of the book and 'made several pregnant suggestions'. Churchill added, 'I cannot help getting very interested in the book. It is a great chance to put my whole case in an agreeable form to an attentive audience.' Gradually the scope of the work widened, for, as he wrote to his wife, 'the more I do, the more I feel the need of doing'. What Churchill had begun as 'a volume of my war memoirs' eventually became a six volume history of the war, *The World Crisis*. The first volume was published in 1923; the last volume, *The Eastern Front*, was published in 1931.

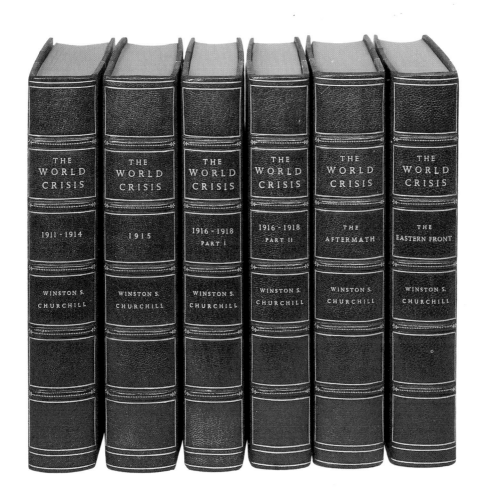

The Cartoonists' Friend

As a member of Lloyd George's peacetime Government, Churchill was a popular figure with the cartoonists. His blunt criticisms of the Labour Party were a frequent subject for their pens. So too was his well-known habit of working in bed.

Churchill himself wrote: 'I always loved cartoons. At my private school at Brighton there were three or four volumes of cartoons from *Punch*, and on Sundays we were allowed to study them. This was a very good way of learning history, or at any rate of learning something. Here, week after week, all the salient events of the world were portrayed in caricature, sometimes grave and sometimes gay.'

'I suppose', Churchill later reflected, 'that long after I have passed beyond the pens of cartoonists my son will have to write and answer letters, saying that my nose was not like a wart, and my hats were fitted by one of the best hatters in London.'

FACING PAGE A Low cartoon published in the *Star* on 21 January 1920.

BELOW A Low cartoon published in the *Star* on 10 May 1922.

82

WINSTON'S BAG

HE HUNTS LIONS AND BRINGS HOME DECAYED CATS

Ireland

It was as a result of the request of the Prime Minister, Lloyd George, that for nearly two years Churchill was at the centre of the negotiations which led to the separation of southern Ireland from the north. It was a time of many conferences, and long debates, leading to the Irish Treaty. It was also a time of danger. In June 1921 one of the strongest critics of the Irish Treaty, Sir Henry Wilson, was assassinated. Churchill had known Wilson well for nearly twenty years, and was one of the principal mourners at his funeral. The police believed that Churchill himself might also become a victim of a murder plot. His car was armoured, a detective accompanied him wherever he went, and he made sure that one of his own pistols was ready for use, if needed.

In August 1922 the leading Irish negotiator of the Treaty, Michael Collins, was murdered. But the Treaty survived, and the Irish Free State came into being. Shortly before his death, Collins sent a message to London: 'Tell Winston we could never have done anything without him.'

BELOW Michael Collins (centre), a photograph taken in March 1922, five months before his assassination.

FACING PAGE Churchill at the State Funeral of Sir Henry Wilson, held at St Paul's Cathedral on 26 June 1922.

Out of Parliament

In October 1922 Lloyd George's Government fell from power, and a General Election was called. During the crisis which led up to the election, Churchill was taken ill with appendicitis, and when he spoke in his constituency at Dundee, on the eve of the poll, he was still in considerable pain.

As a result of the election, the Government was defeated. So too was Churchill at Dundee. For the first time in more than twenty years, he was out of Parliament. As he commented, wrily: 'In the twinkling of an eye I found myself without an office, without a seat, without a party and without an appendix.'

Churchill being helped in Dundee, on the way to speak at the eve of poll meeting in his constituency on 11 November 1922; on his left is his detective, W. H. Thompson, who had been with him since the assassination of Sir Henry Wilson four months before.

LEFT Stanley Baldwin wondering whether to woo Churchill, a cartoon in the *Daily Express*, 26 July 1924.

BELOW Baldwin succumbs, the *Daily Express* two days later.

BELOW RIGHT Churchill during the General Election campaign on 2 October 1924, when he was elected to Parliament for Epping, after an absence of two years.

Return to Parliament

For two years, Churchill was out of Parliament. He was busy, writing his memoirs of the First World War, speaking, and trying to get back into Parliament. In March 1924 he was narrowly beaten for the Abbey Division of Westminster, where he stood as an independent candidate. Shortly afterwards, the Conservative leader, Stanley Baldwin, welcomed Churchill back to the Conservative Party, despite the hostility to Churchill of the Conservative Party 'diehards'. In October 1924 Churchill stood for Parliament again, this time for Epping. Although he called himself a 'Constitutionalist' candidate, he was fully supported by the Conservatives, and was elected to Parliament with a large majority.

Enter The Majority!

DOWN WESTMINSTER WAY, DECEMBER 9th !

BY BLAM

90

Chancellor of the Exchequer

After the Conservatives had won the General Election in October 1924, Stanley Baldwin became Prime Minister. He at once asked Churchill to become Chancellor of the Exchequer, and for nearly five years, Churchill was responsible for the Government's economic policy.

On becoming Chancellor, Churchill and his family moved into the Chancellor's official residence, No. 11 Downing Street, next door to the Prime Minister. It was from No. 11 that Churchill left to go to Parliament, to deliver each of his five budgets.

In 1926, during the General Strike, Churchill edited the Government's newspaper, the *British Gazette*, in which he warned that 'either the country will break the General Strike, or the General Strike will break the country'. Yet despite the Strike, Churchill added, 'The nation remains calm and confident, and the people are bearing with fortitude and good temper the inestimable hardships of a national crisis.'

FACING PAGE A cartoon published in the *Bystander* on 3 December 1924; Austen Chamberlain, the new Foreign Secretary, is on a white horse next to Churchill; Stanley Baldwin (with pipe) leads on a brown horse; Churchill's friend, Lord Birkenhead, newly appointed Secretary of State for India, is on the black horse, smoking the cigar; on the far right (with the black tie) is the Minister of Health, Neville Chamberlain.

BELOW Churchill on his way to the House of Commons to deliver his first budget speech, on 28 April 1925.

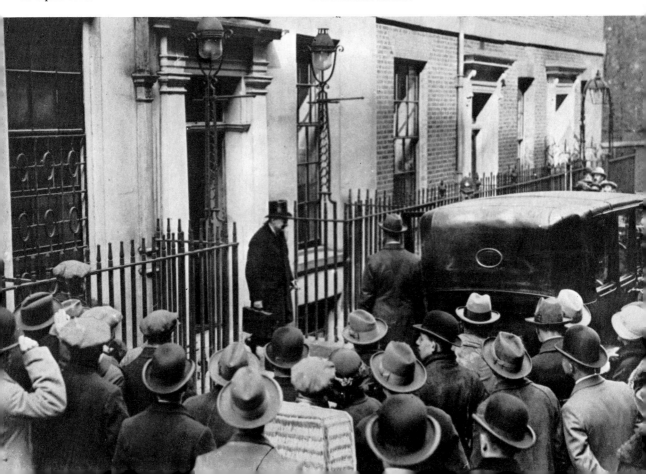

Relaxation

For his winter and summer holidays, Churchill enjoyed above all going to France, where several of his friends had homes and villas. In the 1920s he would often visit his friend the Duke of Westminster at Mimizan, south of Bordeaux.

Whenever Churchill went to France, he set up his easel, and painted. Indeed, for more than forty-five years, painting was both his principal hobby, and his main relaxation. As he himself wrote, in a magazine article in 1925: 'Painting is a companion with whom one may hope to walk a great part of life's journey. One by one the more vigorous sports and exacting games fall away. Exceptional exertions are purchased only by a more pronounced and more prolonged fatigue. Muscles may relax, and feet and hands slow down; the nerve of youth and manhood may become less trusty. But painting is a friend who makes no undue demands, excites to no exhausting pursuits, keeps faithful pace even with feeble steps, and holds her canvas as a screen between us and the envious eyes of Time or the surly advance of Decrepitude. Happy are the painters, for they shall not be lonely. Light and colour, peace and hope, will keep them company to the end, or almost to the end, of the day.'

Churchill painting.

A 1927 portrait of Churchill by Walter Richard
Sickert. During 1927 Sickert taught Churchill the
'panafieu technique' of painting in oils over an
image projected from a photographic plate.

Chartwell

In 1922 Churchill had bought a country house in Kent, Chartwell Manor, and by the time he became Chancellor of the Exchequer at the end of 1924, Chartwell had become his home. Henceforth, for forty years, he was to go down to Chartwell as often as he could, often for months at a time, to work, to relax, to swim, to paint, to write books, to prepare speeches, and to be with his wife, his family and his friends.

BELOW Chartwell, as seen from the South.

FACING PAGE Churchill's study at Chartwell.

Budget Humour

Churchill presented his fourth budget in April 1928. In the four months leading up to it, he was the most cartooned man in Britain, as much so as at any time in his career. In his budget, he aimed at a revival of British industry by bringing to an end all industrial rates. After the budget was over, his cousin Freddie Guest wrote to him: 'I think it will rank as a "classic" budget. It has broken new ground. It will be known as "Winston's industrial life-buoy" and will become a milestone in the history of Reconstructions. I think also you have made many thoughtful friends of crossbench

mind. . . . The press tributes are sincere and have a non-party atmosphere that I like. It seems to me that you have taken a sure step towards your future premiership.'

FACING PAGE Churchill preparing his Fourth Budget, a Bernard Partridge cartoon which appeared in *Punch* on 18 April 1928, six days before Budget Day.

BELOW Churchill as Chancellor of the Exchequer; Low's perspective shows Churchill's past career, at the Colonial Office – green, at the Admiralty – blue, at the Air Ministry – grey, and at the War Office – red.

ST. WINSTON AND THE BRITISH LION.

MR. PUNCH PRESENTS THE ABOVE CARTOON IN CELEBRATION OF THE FOURTH
CENTENARY OF THE DEATH OF ALBRECHT DÜRER.

The Smiling Chancellor

Churchill's five years as Chancellor of the Exchequer were a happy time for him. The Prime Minister, Stanley Baldwin, often sought his advice and counsel. He had become increasingly popular in the Conservative Party. His speeches in Parliament were hailed even by his severest critics as masterpieces of oratory, and of humour.

By the time of his last budget, in April 1929, Churchill was fifty-four years old.

Considering the many controversies of the past, his political career had clearly reached a high point, possibly its highest point. His literary career also flourished, as he continued to publish his history of the First World War, and began to plan yet another ambitious work, a biography of his ancestor John Churchill, the first Duke of Marlborough.

After Churchill had introduced his last budget, one of his Cabinet colleagues, Neville Chamberlain, wrote in his diary that Churchill's speech 'was one of the best he has made, and kept the House fascinated by its wit, audacity, adroitness and power'.

ABOVE Stanley Baldwin and Churchill.

FACING PAGE Churchill leaving 11 Downing Street on 15 April 1929, on his way to deliver his fifth Budget; with him is his wife, his son, Randolph, then aged seventeen, his Private Secretary Robert Boothby (in top hat) and his fourteen-year-old daughter Sarah (partly hidden).

5

The Wilderness Years
1929-1939

In June 1929 the Conservatives were defeated at the general election, Churchill was no longer Chancellor of the Exchequer. Instead, a Labour Government came to power, headed by Ramsay MacDonald.

What was Churchill's future to be? A year earlier a magazine writer had reflected, on Churchill: 'Some say that he can never achieve the Premiership, because he is not a strong enough Party man. But politics are in a fluid state just now. Strange winds are blowing up. The political pilots are apprehensive and perplexed. It is yet possible that a great and sudden wave will obliterate old landmarks and personalities, and sweep the astonishing Winston Churchill on its foaming crest to the Premiership'.

The political crisis came in 1931, with the growing economic troubles, following the 'Great Crash'. But Churchill was no longer in a position to gain office. He had quarrelled with the Conservative Party leaders. The cause of this quarrel was Baldwin's decision to support the Labour Party's policy of eventual self-government for India.

MacDonald and Baldwin made common cause. In August 1931, a National Government was set up, with MacDonald as Prime Minister, and Baldwin as his second-in-command. Churchill was not invited to join the new Cabinet. And at the General Election two months later, the National Government received a massive majority. MacDonald remained Prime Minister, with the Conservatives holding by far the largest number of Parliamentary seats and Cabinet posts. Churchill remained in the 'wilderness'.

FACING PAGE Churchill lunching with one of his publishers, George Harrap.

PLEASURE ISLAND:

BEING A PLAN IN THE OLD MANNER OF THE LAKE ISLAND IN CANADA WHICH
MR. WINSTON CHURCHILL IS SAID TO COVET.

Travels in the New World

Following the defeat of the Conservative Government in 1929, Churchill took a prolonged holiday in Canada and the United States. Once more, he set up his easel wherever he went, and painted the new scenes. He was actually in New York during the 'Great Crash', when the financial stability of the United States seemed suddenly at risk. 'Under my window', he wrote, 'a gentleman cast himself down fifteen storeys, and was dashed to pieces'.

But Churchill retained his faith in the eventual recovery of the finances of the United States, reflecting, in an article which he wrote on his return to England, that the financial disaster, 'cruel as it is to thousands, is only a passing episode in the march of a valiant and serviceable people who by fierce experiment are hewing new paths for man, and show-ing to all nations much that they should attempt and much that they should avoid'.

FACING PAGE A cartoon by L. Raven-Hill, published in *Punch* on 11 September 1929.

BELOW A photograph of Lake Louise in the Canadian Rockies. Churchill painted this scene in 1929.

Accident and Recovery

In 1930 Churchill was made Chancellor of Bristol University. To mark the occasion he was placed 'under arrest' by students of the university. They had found him 'guilty' of 'acquiring a new hat and a new chancellorship and with neglecting to supply morning coffee and biscuits to the students'. Carried shoulder high by the students he bore his 'arrest' bravely and continued to smoke his cigar. A year later, in New York, while crossing the road, he was hit by a car and severely injured. While recovering, he once more set up his easel and painted.

FACING PAGE Churchill 'under arrest' at Bristol.

RIGHT Churchill leaving hospital in New York on 21 December 1931, eight days after being knocked down by a car in Fifth Avenue; with him is his detective, W. H. Thompson.

BELOW Blenheim Palace under snow. Here Churchill was born, and here in 1930 he commenced research for his book *Marlborough: His Life and Times*.

Illness and Recuperation

In 1932 Churchill was again seriously ill, having caught paratyphoid while travelling in Germany and Austria, working on his new book, the life of his ancestor, John Churchill, first Duke of Marlborough. After his return from the nursing home, he began once more to dictate further chapters. But he was again taken ill, and for many months was too weak to take part in politics. He recovered slowly, painting, and continuing with his *Marlborough: His Life and Times*. He also signed a contract, at the end of 1932, to write yet another book, a *History of the English Speaking Peoples*, for which he was to receive £20,000. As Churchill busied himself writing, his secretary wrote to a friend: 'Mr Churchill is steadily improving, though progress is rather slow, but as usual nothing can keep him from work.'

BELOW Churchill leaving a London nursing home on 10 October 1932 after he had been taken ill with paratyphoid.

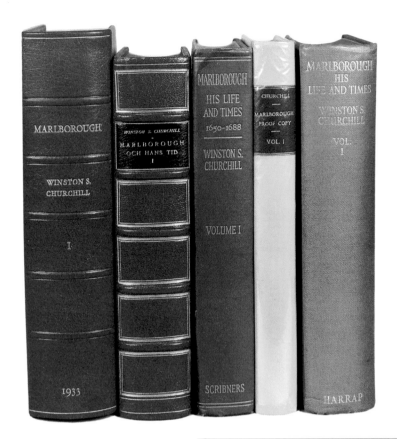

ABOVE Various editions of Churchill's
Marlborough: His Life and Times. From left to
right: the de luxe edition of 1933, one hundred
and fifty autographed copies of which were
published; a Swedish edition, which was
presented to Churchill by the Swedish publisher
in December 1940; the first American edition: a
proof copy, which Churchill used for corrections
and indexing; and the first English edition, which
was published in 1933.

RIGHT The Great Democracies, volume four of a
History of the English Speaking Peoples. Churchill
began this work in 1936, but it was not published
until 1956. In the preface of the book, Churchill
explained the delay of over twenty years: 'During
nearly six years of war, and an even longer period
in which I was writing my war memoirs, the book
slumbered peacefully. It is only now when things
have settled down that I present to the public a
History of the English Speaking Peoples.'

ABOVE LEFT Professor Lindemann.

ABOVE Brendan Bracken.

LEFT Major Desmond Morton.

Friends and Allies

Throughout his ten years in the political 'wilderness', Churchill was offered no place in the Cabinet. But a small group of friends still believed that the time would come when he would be called back to office.

Each of Churchill's friends encouraged him to continue with his warnings. Professor Lindemann, from Oxford, gave him advice on all scientific developments; Brendan Bracken, a young Conservative M.P., kept him in touch with the daily shifts and changes of the Parliamentary scene; and Desmond Morton, the head of one of the Government's own intelligence agencies, provided Churchill from week to week with the facts about German and British military production.

Twice a year, Churchill would go to France for his holidays. Here he found, while painting and writing in the homes of friends, the peace of mind which he needed to give him strength to continue with the uphill fight to alert the British Government, and the British people, to the ever-growing danger of Nazi Germany.

Churchill walking in the grounds of Chartwell with his friend Ralph Wigram, a senior Foreign Office official who shared Churchill's mistrust of Nazi Germany.

Reflections and Expectations

In July 1934 one of Churchill's closest friends died. This was his cousin 'Sunny', the 9th Duke of Marlborough, whose company he had enjoyed since their childhood days, more than fifty years earlier. It was a time of sad reflection for Churchill himself, now approaching his own sixtieth birthday.

Of his cousin's death, Churchill wrote: 'Sunny did not inquire too closely about the symptoms which daily struck him new blows. He took the best advice, and lived his life without unduly focusing on the future. But he knew quite well that his end was approaching, that he was, as he said, at the end of his tether. He faced this universal ordeal with dignity and simplicity, making neither too much nor too little of it. He always had the most attractive and graceful manners and that easy courtesy we have been taught by the gentlefolk of a bygone age. At a tea party, to some of those who cared about him, on the last night of his life, when strength had almost ebbed away, he was concerned with the entertainment of his guests, and that his conversation had not been wearisome to them. Then came that good gift of the gods to those in such straits, sleep from which in this world there is no awakening.'

Churchill at the funeral of his cousin, the 9th Duke of Marlborough.

110

Four months after his cousin's death, Churchill went with his wife on a cruise to the eastern Mediterranean. At each port of call he painted, as well as writing further newspaper articles.

Churchill was now winning an ever widening public for his views on the dangers of Nazism, despite the unpopularity of these views in political circles. Indeed, during 1934, a leading Edinburgh businessman wrote to him: 'In these confused and confusing days I doubt if you know how frequently in ordinary experience men seem to turn half expectantly to you. Your detachment from politics recently, the compelling merit of what you have written added to your own signal achievements prior to and during the war have created an expectancy.'

Wing Commander Torr Anderson, an officer who gave Churchill secret information about air force deficiencies.

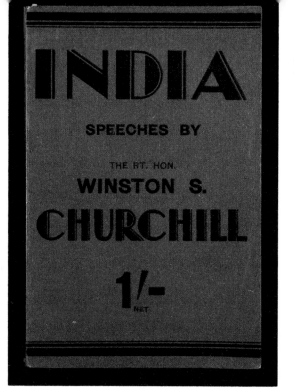

India

For five years, Churchill challenged the Government's decision to give self-government to India. He did not believe that India could survive as a united country, or be ruled with fairness to all classes, once Britain gave up its power. More than a hundred Conservative M.P.S supported Churchill in his opposition to their Party's policy. But this dividing of the Party created a feeling of deep anger among the leaders, and seriously lessened the chance of Churchill being brought into the Cabinet. At the same time, his strenuous efforts to warn the country of what he saw as the dangers of self-government for India seemed, to some, to blunt the edge of his equally strenuous efforts to warn about the Nazi danger.

ABOVE In May 1935, as part of his own campaign, Churchill published his speeches on India in book form.

BELOW Churchill's son Randolph stood for Parliament in opposition – like his father – to the India Bill; Randolph was defeated; this cartoon by Low was published on 1 March 1935 in the *Eastern Evening News*.

Friday   EASTERN EVENING NEWS   March 1, 1935

BY-ELECTION SUPPORT FOR THE CHURCHILL PARTY

(Copyright in all countries)

112

A cartoon published in the *Tatler* on 18 December 1935.

LIKE FATHER, LIKE SON? (No. XI)

MR. WINSTON CHURCHILL AND MR. RANDOLPH CHURCHILL

By TONY WYSARD

One might almost add " Like Grandfather . . ." for ever since the days of the late Lord Randolph the name of Churchill has meant a great deal in political circles. History and irreverent cartoonists have between them associated Mr. Winston Churchill with such diverse matters as funny hats, Sidney Street, the Cabinet, water-colour painting, and, of course, the very vexed question of India, and once again we find him representing the Epping Division of Essex under the new Government. It will be interesting to see how far in his father's footsteps Mr. Randolph Churchill manages to follow

Air Defence

After Hitler came to power in Germany in January 1933, Churchill's main worry about British defence was the problem of weakness in the air. Only a strong British air force, he believed, could protect Britain from invasion and defeat, or from being blackmailed by Germany. Although the German air force in 1934 was still a small one, he warned that it would soon outstrip Britain's, both in numbers of aeroplanes, and in their quality.

One of Churchill's main informants about Britain's air weakness was a brave and distinguished pilot, Squadron Leader Torr Anderson, who for three years provided Churchill with many secret details of aircraft construction and policy. Another informant was a young official at the Foreign Office, Ralph Wigram, who, like Anderson, would visit Churchill with documents and materials which Churchill then studied, and used in his speeches. When Wigram died in 1936, at the age of forty-six, Churchill wrote to his widow: 'I always admired so much his courage, integrity of purpose, high comprehending vision. He was one of those – how few – who guard the life of Britain. Now he is gone.'

BELOW Hitler with other Nazi leaders, a photograph taken at Kiel in 1933.

FACING PAGE Churchill was accused of having a 'bee in his bonnet' about air defences and German air strength; this cartoon by Cecil Orr was published in the *Daily Record and Mail* on 28 November 1934; Hitler's face appeared as the propeller.

Air-Minded

The Gathering Storm

In May 1937 Neville Chamberlain became Prime Minister. But there was still no place for Churchill in the Cabinet, despite a growing public feeling that his warnings about Germany had been justified, and that his experience and energy would both be important assets at a time of growing danger.

Although Churchill now had a flat in London, where he stayed when Parliament was in session, he lived mostly at Chartwell, finishing the last chapters of his four-volume *Life of Marlborough*, painting, writing newspaper articles, and preparing a series of speeches. In one of these speeches he spoke against the German persecution of the Jews. 'It is a horrible thing', he said, 'that a race of people should be attempted to be blotted out of the society in which they have been born', and he went on to warn against Neville Chamberlain's policy of appeasement, telling the House of Commons: 'If it were thought that we were making terms for ourselves at the expense either of small nations or of large conceptions which are dear, not only to many nations, but

to millions of people in every nation, a knell of despair would resound through many parts of Europe.'

In December 1937 General Ironside had a long talk with Churchill. In his diary, Ironside wrote, of Churchill: 'His energy and fiery brain seem unimpaired with age. He is certainly not dismayed by our difficulties. He says that our rulers are now beginning to get frightened. . . . He says that sometimes he couldn't sleep at night thinking of our dangers, how all this wonderful Empire which had been built up so slowly and so steadily might all be dissipated in a minute.'

FACING PAGE Churchill signing autographs during the Conservative Party Conference at Scarborough on 7 October 1937.

BELOW The front entrance at Chartwell, a photograph taken during the 1930s.

The Year of Munich

Throughout 1938, Churchill urged the British Government to be prepared to support the small state of Czechoslovakia against German aggression. But Neville Chamberlain preferred to reach a direct agreement with Germany, hoping to prevent war by a policy of compromise. After the Munich agreement had been signed, and Czechoslovakia had been forced to give up some of its territory to Hitler, Churchill told the House of Commons: 'What I find unendurable is the sense of our country falling into the power, into the orbit and influence of Nazi Germany, and of our existence becoming dependent upon their good will or pleasure. It is to prevent that that I have tried my best to urge the maintenance of every bulwark of defence – first the timely creation of an Air Force superior to anything within striking distance of our shores; secondly the gathering together of the collective strength of many nations; and thirdly, the making of alliances and military conventions, all within the Covenant, in order to gather together forces at any rate to restrain the onward movement of Nazi power. It has all been in vain. Every position has been successively undermined and abandoned on specious and plausible excuses.'

FACING PAGE Churchill at Versailles on 23 July 1938, during the State Visit to France of King George VI and Queen Elizabeth.

RIGHT Churchill in Paris on 21 September 1938, during the Munich crisis, with his friend and literary agent Dr Emery Reves.

BELOW Neville Chamberlain and Mussolini at the Munich Conference, 30 September 1938.

Towards War

For the first six months of 1939, Churchill pressed the Government to take more active measures in case of a possible war with Germany. The Government, however, still rejected his advice, and individual Cabinet ministers continued to belittle his judgment. After the German occupation of Prague in March 1939, the Press began to call, with increasing force, for Churchill's return to the Cabinet. Labour, Liberal and Conservative papers all urged the Government to give Churchill a place. Churchill's inclusion in the Cabinet, wrote one newspaper, 'might indeed irritate Hitler. But if we are to leave men out because they are efficient and resolute, we may as well give up the ghost here and now.'

Churchill entertains the former French Prime Minister, Léon Blum, at Chartwell on 10 May 1939; with them are Clementine Churchill (with fox cub,) and Richard Law (son of the former Conservative Prime Minister, Andrew Bonar Law), a Conservative Member of Parliament who had, like Churchill, opposed the Munich agreement.

'Going up', a cartoon published in the *Star* on
5 July 1939; Churchill was well known as an
amateur bricklayer and had built several walls
and a small cottage at Chartwell.

The Eve of War

In August 1939, as the Press demands for Churchill's inclusion in the Government grew louder, Churchill went to visit the defences of the Maginot Line, in eastern France, and to see the border with Germany. A friend who accompanied Churchill wrote in his diary: 'The trip tore to shreds any illusion that it was not Germany's intention to wage war and to wage it soon. There was no mistaking the grim, relentless and barely concealed preparations she was making.' From the Maginot Line, Churchill travelled to Saint-Georges-Motel, a château west of Paris, the home of Consuelo Balsan, whose mill was a familiar subject for his painting. On the day of his arrival at the château, *The Times* published a letter signed by 375 members of the staffs of every British university, 'strongly urging' Churchill's inclusion in the Government.

BELOW Churchill painting at the Mill of Saint-Georges-Motel.

The mill at Château Saint-Georges-Motel. Churchill painted the mill from this angle on one of his many visits there.

The Coming of War, 1939

Painting alongside Churchill at Saint-Georges-Motel in the second week of August 1939 was his friend Paul Maze, a painter whom he had first met on the Western Front in 1916. Paul Maze recorded the day's painting in his diary: 'I worked alongside him. He suddenly turned to me and said: "This is the last picture we shall paint in peace for a very long time." What amazed me was his concentration over his painting. No one but he could have understood more what the possibility of war meant, and how ill-prepared we were. As he worked, he would now and then make statements as to the relative strength of the German Army or the French Army. "They are strong, I tell you, they are strong," he would say. Then his jaw would clench his large cigar, and I felt the determination of his will. "Ah," he would say, "with it all, we shall have him." '

In the third week of August Churchill returned to London, in time for the recall of Parliament. On 1 September 1939 Hitler invaded Poland. The events that Churchill had feared, and forecast, were about to unfold.

Stefan Lorant at Chartwell in February 1939, interviewing Churchill for an article in *Picture Post*, a weekly magazine which called for Churchill's return to the Cabinet throughout the spring and summer of 1939.

NOW THEY LISTEN TO CHURCHILL

Kept out of Conservative Cabinets for years, Winston Churchill comes back as a political power because his warnings proved true.

ABOVE Page three of the *New York Times* magazine on 13 August 1939.

RIGHT The typed notice summoning the House of Commons on 31 August 1939.

On Thursday, 31st August, 1939, the House will meet at 2 45 p m.

Debate on the International situation, and consideration of any necessary emergency business.

Your attendance at 2 45 p.m is particularly requested

DAVID MARGESSON.

NOTE.   IMPORTANT.

In view of the uncertainty of the course of events, the House may be called together before Thursday, 31st August Should this be necessary, it may only be possible to give Members 24 hour's notice.

The Tatler

Vol. CLIII. No. 1993. London, September 6, 1939

POSTAGE: Inland 1½d.; Canada and Newfoundland 1½d.; Foreign 3d.

Price One Shilling

NOT A CABINET PORTRAIT—UNFORTUNATELY

6

Britain Alone

FACING PAGE Churchill
and Anthony Eden on
their way to the House
of Commons, from the
front page of the
Tatler on 6 September
1939, three days after
the British declaration
of war on Germany;
the photograph had
been taken a week
before, when neither
Churchill nor Eden
were in the Cabinet.

On 1 September 1939 Germany invaded Poland, and two days later Britain declared war on Germany. After ten years without political office, Churchill was brought into the Government as First Lord of the Admiralty, the position he had held on the outbreak of war in 1914.

Three months after the outbreak of the Second World War, Churchill reached his sixty-fifth birthday, for many men the age of retirement. But his energy seemed unbounded, and his determination to see Hitler defeated, despite the enormous German superiority, was obvious to all.

With the German invasion of France, Belgium and Holland on 10 May 1940, Churchill succeeded Neville Chamberlain as Prime Minister. It was a bleak time for Britain. After the German conquest of France, all Europe lay under Nazi rule or influence. Stalin had made his peace with Hitler. The United States remained neutral. The German air bombardment of Britain, the 'Blitz', seemed a prelude to invasion.

During this perilous time, Churchill broadcast words of courage, and of confidence. His War Cabinet, in which the Labour Party was strongly represented, directed the war from day to day, under Churchill's constant and sharp scrutiny.

By the end of 1940, despite all Hitler's efforts, Britain was still capable of waging war, of defending itself in the air, and of fighting back against the submarine peril at sea. As Churchill himself wrote: 'Alone, but upborne by every generous heart-beat of mankind, we had defied the tyrant in his hour of triumph.'

Nr. 39 — 92. Jahrg.
Berlin, 24. September 1939

Preis **30** Pfg.

Kladderadatsch

Churchill, der Puppenspieler

The Admiralty

On Churchill's arrival at the Admiralty in September 1939, a message was sent out to all ships: 'Winston is back.' Indeed, Churchill's return was greeted with general rejoicing by the British people. President Roosevelt was also pleased, writing to Churchill in November 1939: 'It is because you and I occupied similar positions in the First World War that I want you to know how glad I am that you are back again in the Admiralty.' From the Germans, however, Churchill's return to the Cabinet provoked an outburst of fury.

Churchill now settled down to heavy responsibilities, interrupted only briefly for his son's wedding. Nor did he see any immediate cause for optimism. 'So far no ally had espoused our cause', he wrote of the new year, 1940. 'The United States was cooler than in any other period. I persevered in my correspondence with the President, but with little response.'

FACING PAGE 'Churchill the Puppet master', a German cartoon published on 24 September 1939; Churchill in Admiral's uniform has just dropped the Foreign Secretary, Lord Halifax, on the floor and is holding the Prime Minister, Neville Chamberlain, in his left hand.

BELOW Churchill leaves his London flat for his son's wedding on 4 October 1939; trying to fight a way to the car door is his detective, W. H. Thompson, who was to remain at Churchill's side throughout the Second World War.

Growing Responsibilities

As a member of Neville Chamberlain's small War Cabinet, Churchill was soon asked to undertake wider responsibilities. In January 1940 he visited France, and discussed the problems of the defence of French soil with General Georges, the French general who had shown him around the Maginot Line only five months before, in peacetime, when he was in the political wilderness. It was also while he was at the Admiralty that Churchill set up his own statistical department headed by his friend Professor Lindemann, to cast a critical eye on all the claims and counter-claims of war production and experiment.

But Churchill was worried, as he wrote to one Cabinet colleague, on his return from France in January 1940, that all the various war projects being discussed 'will succumb before the tremendous array of negative argument and forces'. For this was the time of the 'phoney war', when Hitler, having conquered Poland, made no move against the west. Warsaw, the Polish capital, had been severely bombed. But as yet no German bombs had fallen on Britain or France.

In February 1940, Chamberlain invited Churchill to join the Supreme War Council, the aim of which was to co-ordinate British and French war policy. In April he was appointed head of the Military Co-ordination Committee, to link together the plans and operations of the Admiralty, the War Office and the Air Ministry. But he was not satisfied with the system, which produced, he wrote, 'a copious flow of polite conversation', but no real decisions.

BELOW Neville Chamberlain's War Cabinet, a photograph taken on 8 November 1939; back row: Sir Kingsley Wood, Churchill, Leslie Hore-Belisha and Lord Hankey; seated: Lord Halifax, Sir John Simon, Neville Chamberlain, Sir Samuel Hoare and Lord Chatfield.

FACING PAGE Churchill in France in January 1940, talking to General Georges.

130

Prime Minister

In the early hours of 10 May 1940 the German armies invaded France, Belgium and Holland. The 'phoney war' was over. The British troops in France prepared to join battle with the advancing German forces. That same evening Churchill succeeded Chamberlain as Prime Minister.

Within a few hours, Churchill had formed his War Cabinet, bringing in the leaders of the Labour Party to high office, their first share of government for nearly ten years. Sir Archibald Sinclair, his former adjutant, and now leader of the Liberal Party, went to the Air Ministry, and Anthony Eden to the War Office. Churchill himself assumed the additional office of Minister of Defence.

'... as I went to bed at about 3 a.m., I was conscious of a profound sense of relief. At last I had the authority to give directions over the whole scene. I felt as if I were walking with destiny, and that all my past life had been but a preparation for this hour and for this trial. Eleven years in the political wilderness had freed me from ordinary Party antagonisms. My warnings over the last six years had been so numerous, so detailed and were now so terribly vindicated, that no one could gainsay me. I could not be reproached either for making the war or with want of preparation for it. I thought I knew a good deal about it all, and I was sure I should not fail. Therefore, although impatient for the morning, I slept soundly and had no need for cheering dreams. Facts are better than dreams.'

Churchill, Prime Minister, since 10 May 1940, leaves Admiralty House two days later, on his way to Buckingham Palace.

A cartoon published on 8 June 1940 in the *Daily Express.*

The Eve of Invasion

The German advance across the Low Countries and France was swift and brutal. After ten days, on 15 May 1940, the Dutch Army surrendered, following a severe German air attack on Rotterdam. At a special service in Westminster Abbey on 26 May 1940 Churchill shared what he described as 'the fear of the congregation, not of death or wounds or material loss, but of defeat and the final ruin of Britain'. On the following day the Belgian Army capitulated, and on 14 June the Germans entered Paris. France sued for an armistice, and German troops occupied the Channel ports. From Calais, the Germans could see Dover.

Churchill and his Government began at once to prepare to meet a German invasion. When it would come, they could not tell; that it would come seemed certain.

LEFT German troops enter Paris on 14 June 1940.

FACING PAGE Churchill's letter, sent to all senior civil servants on 4 July 1940.

10, DOWNING STREET,
WHITEHALL.

ON what may be the eve of an attempted invasion or battle for our native land, the Prime Minister desires to impress upon all persons holding responsible positions in the Government, in the Fighting Services, or in the Civil Departments, their duty to maintain a spirit of alert and confident energy. While every precaution must be taken that time and means afford, there are no grounds for supposing that more German troops can be landed in this country, either from the air or across the sea, than can be destroyed or captured by the strong forces at present under arms. The Royal Air Force is in excellent order and at the highest strength it has yet attained. The German Navy was never so weak, nor the British Army at home so strong as now. The Prime Minister expects all His Majesty's servants in high places to set an example of steadiness and resolution. They should check and rebuke expressions of loose and ill-digested opinion in their circles, or by their subordinates. They should not hesitate to report, or if necessary remove, any officers or officials who are found to be consciously exercising a disturbing or depressing influence, and whose talk is calculated to spread alarm and despondency. Thus alone will they be worthy of the fighting men, who in the air, on the sea, and on land, have already met the enemy without any sense of being out-matched in martial qualities.

Winston S. Churchill

4th July, 1940.

135

The Blitz

No invasion took place; instead, in September 1940, the Germans launched a massive air attack on London and the principal British cities. Within eight months, more than 60,000 civilians had been killed, and large parts of several cities had been reduced to rubble.

The ferocity of the Blitz led to no weakening of British resolve. The fighter pilots fought to destroy as many of the attacking bombers as possible, destroying fifty-six in a single day. At the same time, the Royal Air Force struck as far east as they were able, bombing Berlin on the night of 23 September, while London itself was still being bombed.

On 8 October 1940 Churchill told the House of Commons: 'No one can predict, no one can even imagine, how this terrible war against German and Nazi aggression will run its course or how far it will spread or how long it will last. Not only great dangers, but many more misfortunes, many shortcomings, many mistakes, many disappointments will surely be our lot. Death and sorrow will be the companions of our journey; hardship our garment; constancy and valour our only shield. We must be united, we must be undaunted, we must be inflexible. Our qualities and deeds must burn and glow through the gloom of Europe until they become the veritable beacon of its salvation.'

BELOW King George VI points out to Churchill the bomb damage at Buckingham Palace on 1 September 1940.

RIGHT On 15 September 1940, at the height of the blitz, the scoreboard in Churchill's underground headquarters gives the estimated numbers of German aircraft losses.

BELOW The invasion threat is beaten back, a cartoon by E. H. Shepherd published in *Punch* on 25 September 1940.

Help from the United States

Throughout his first year as Prime Minister, the importance of obtaining military supplies from the United States was uppermost in Churchill's mind. In July 1940 he appealed to Roosevelt for '50 or 60 of your oldest destroyers', and when Roosevelt agreed to send this small but much needed assistance, Churchill replied that 'the moral value of this fresh aid from your Government and people at this critical time will be very great and widely felt'.

Two months later, Roosevelt released 250,000 American rifles for Britain's urgent needs.

Thus began the slow but steady process which reached its climax in March 1941, with the United States' vast 'Lease-Lend' programme, which Churchill described as 'the most unsordid act in the history of any nation'.

BELOW Churchill and his ADC, Commander 'Tommy' Thompson, in January 1941, with President Roosevelt's personal emissary, Harry Hopkins, who was about to return to the United States on board the battleship *King George V*.

FACING PAGE Churchill watches the arrival of the first aircraft from the United States under the 'Lease-Lend' programme.

OUTWARD TELEGRAM

PRIME MINISTER'S

PERSONAL TELEGRAM

[Cypher].   SPECIAL (P.M.T.)

SERIAL No. T 230

FROM FOREIGN OFFICE TO WASHINGTON.

No. 2909.   D. 4.05 p.m.   29th May, 1941.
29th May, 1941.

                        eeeeeeeee

        The following message has been sent by former Naval
person to President Roosevelt through United States
Embassy.

        (Begins).

        We are uplifted and fortified by your memorable
declaration and by the far-reaching executive measures
involved in the state of emergency you have proclaimed.
Pray accept, Mr. President, my heartfelt thanks. It was
very kind of you to let me know beforehand of the great
advance you found it possible to make.

        I have now also received your message about the impressive
additional output you are sending to the Middle East in
United States ships. Winant will tell you what I managed
to send out there secretly and the hopes I have of some
good news coming to hand before long.

        It seems most important to find the Prinz Eugen before
she cuts into our convoys. The Admiralty and Ghormley
are in the closest touch. But this is a new, very fast
and powerful ship, and there is much danger while she is
at large for any convoy unprotected by battleship escort.

        I will send you later the inside story of the
fighting with the Bismarck. She was a terrific ship and
a masterpiece of naval construction. Her removal eases
our battleship situation as we should have to keep K.G.V.,
Prince of Wales and the two Nelsons practically tied to
Scapa Flow to guard against a sortie of Bismarck and
Tirpitz as they could choose their moment and we should
have to allow for one of our ships refitting. Now it is
a different story. The effect upon the Japanese will be
highly beneficial. I expect they are doing all their
sums again.

                        (Ends).

7

The Grand Alliance

FACING PAGE
Churchill's personal
telegram to Roosevelt
on 29 May 1941.

In June 1941 Hitler invaded Russia; now Stalin was Britain's ally. In December 1941 Japan attacked the United States, bringing the vast industrial might and war potential of America into the war. A Grand Alliance was forged, and at times of crisis and disagreement, Churchill made it his business to visit both Roosevelt and Stalin, in an attempt to evolve a united war strategy.

Churchill's wartime journeys took him tens of thousands of miles across the oceans, as far east as Moscow, Teheran and the Crimea. He visited the battle zones in North Africa, in Italy, in France, and even when the war was going badly, or slowly, for the Allies, he brought his message of hope in victory.

Yet when victory came, in May 1945, Churchill had no illusions about the problems that lay ahead, and in his victory broadcast to the British people he declared: 'On the continent of Europe we have yet to make sure that the simple and honourable purposes for which we entered the war are not brushed aside or overlooked in the months following our success, and that the words "freedom", "democracy", and "liberation" are not distorted from their true meaning as we have understood them. There would be little use in punishing the Hitlerites for their crimes if law and justice did not rule, and if totalitarian or police governments were to take the place of the German invaders. We seek nothing for ourselves. But we must make sure that those causes which we fought for find recognition at the peace table in facts as well as words, and above all we must labour to ensure that the World Organization which the United Nations are creating at San Francisco does not become an idle name, does not become a shield for the strong, and a mockery of the weak. It is the victors who must search their hearts in their glowing hours, and be worthy by their nobility of the immense forces that they wield.'

Across the Atlantic

In August 1941 Churchill decided that, although the United States was still neutral, there was much to be gained by a personal meeting with Roosevelt. Travelling on Britain's newest battleship, the *Prince of Wales*, he crossed the Atlantic to Placentia Bay, in Newfoundland, making wide diversions to avoid the many German submarines then active in the North Atlantic.

In order to preserve secrecy during the crossing, almost total radio silence had to be maintained. 'There was thus a lull in my daily routine', Churchill wrote, 'and a strange sense of leisure which I had not known since the war began.'

BELOW Churchill on his way to meet Roosevelt, aboard the battleship *Prince of Wales*.

FACING PAGE Churchill and his friend Lord Beaverbrook, a member of the War Cabinet, leaving the ship during the Atlantic meeting.

Meeting with Roosevelt

The meeting between Churchill and Roosevelt took place on 9 August 1941. During the voyage Churchill had prepared a joint Anglo-American declaration, and this became the basis of the 'Atlantic Charter', pledging the two countries to defend 'the right of freedom of speech and thought', and to set up an international organization which 'will afford to all States and peoples the means of dwelling in security within their own bounds, and of travelling the seas and oceans without fear of lawless assault'.

On Sunday, 10 August, Roosevelt joined Churchill on the *Prince of Wales*, for Divine Service. 'This service', Churchill wrote, 'was felt by us all to be a deeply moving expression of the unity of faith of our two peoples.'

FACING PAGE Churchill and Roosevelt meet on board ship in Placentia Bay, Newfoundland on 9 August 1941; Roosevelt is supported by his son, as Churchill hands him a letter of greeting from the King.

BELOW Divine Service on the *Prince of Wales* on 10 August 1941.

The Widening War

On 7 December 1941 Japanese forces attacked the American air and sea base at Pearl Harbor. At the same time, Hitler declared war on the United States. Britain and America were now Allies, and, together with the Soviet Union, were pledged to defeat Germany by a united effort.

Four days after Pearl Harbor, Churchill set off again across the Atlantic, this time for the United States. For three weeks he stayed at the White House, discussing each day with Roosevelt the strategy of what was now a world war. He visited the United States again, in June, and in August he flew to Moscow for his first meeting with Stalin. The Grand Alliance had been forged.

Churchill in Washington, accompanied by detective Thompson, on his way to address the Joint Session of Congress on 26 December 1941.

Churchill with Stalin on 16 August 1942; Stalin
has signed and dated the photograph.

Wartime Travels

Throughout 1942 and 1943, Churchill, now sixty-eight years old, travelled widely in order to co-ordinate the war policies of the Allied powers, and to discuss the strategy of the war with the political and military leaders. In August 1942, after leaving Moscow, he had gone to Cairo. In January 1943 he was in Casablanca, in May in Washington, in June in Algiers, in November in Teheran, and in December in Cairo again. Tiring though these journeys were, they made it possible for Churchill to keep in close touch with the political and military leaders, and to resolve many complex problems.

Churchill visiting the desert front west of Cairo in August 1942.

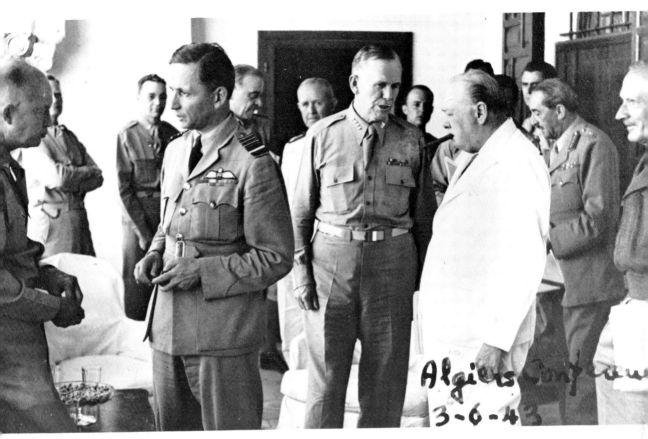

Algiers Conference
3-6-43

ABOVE Churchill at the Algiers Conference on 3 June 1943; from left to right: General Eisenhower, Air Marshal Tedder, General Marshall, General Sir Alan Brooke and General Montgomery, whose handwriting is on the photograph.

As he travelled, Churchill found many opportunities to visit the troops. On one of his trips to Cairo in 1942 he was surprised at the scanty dress of the British soldiers, as he recalled in his memoirs: 'When I marched to Omdurman forty-four years before, the theory was that the African sun must at all cost be kept away from the skin. . . . Yet now half way through the twentieth century many of the white soldiers went about their daily toil hatless and naked except for the equal of a loin cloth. Apparently it did them no harm.'

ABOVE The *Queen Mary* (84,000 tons) in a gale 500 miles west of Ireland whilst on passage to Halifax with Churchill and his staff on board.

Storms and Sickness

As the wartime conferences continued, so too did Churchill's travelling. In August 1943 he again travelled to Canada to finalize at Quebec the plans for the 'D-Day' landings. The journey across the Atlantic, on the *Queen Mary*, was so stormy that the escorts found it difficult to keep their stations. From Quebec, Churchill went on to Washington, returning to England in the battleship *Renown*.

In October 1943 Churchill met Stalin again at Teheran, and then flew to Cairo for a further conference with Roosevelt. After Cairo, he flew to Tunis, intent on flying on to visit the troops on the Italian front. But on his arrival at Tunis in mid-December he was taken seriously ill with pneumonia. His recovery was slow, and it was more than a month before he was well enough to return to England.

LEFT Churchill in Tunis, recovering from his illness in December 1943.

FACING PAGE One of Clementine Churchill's wartime Christmas cards.

Christmas Wishes from
Clementine S.
Churchill

D-Day

The climax of Churchill's hopes and plans came on 6 June 1944, 'D-Day', with the launching of Operation Overlord. Now at last the German mastery of Europe was to be challenged by a direct and massive assault.

On 'D-Day' plus six, 12 June 1944, Churchill himself crossed the Channel to France, in the destroyer *Kelvin*, watching from the bridge of the ship while it bombarded the German positions. Then he went ashore, greeted by General Montgomery, and for seven hours drove through the battle zone, and made a thirty-

mile tour of the liberated coastline before returning to England.

In July Churchill returned to France, where he opened the 'Winston' bridge over the River Orne, at Caen.

BELOW Churchill crossing the River Orne with Generals Montgomery and Dempsey.

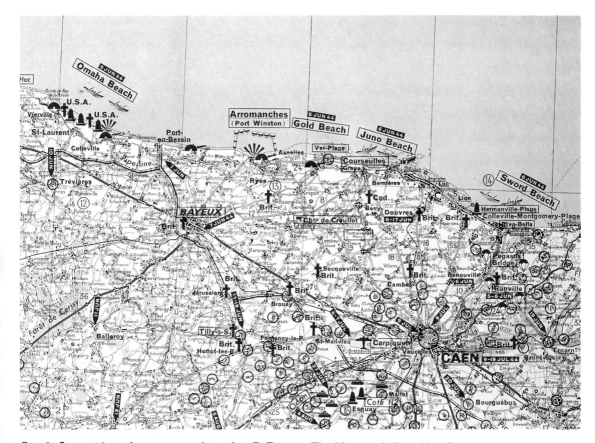

The Normandy beachhead.

On 6 June 1944, in announcing the D-Day landings to the House of Commons, Churchill said: 'The battle that has now begun will grow constantly in scale and in intensity for many weeks to come, and I shall not attempt to speculate upon its course. This I may say however. Complete unity prevails throughout the Allied Armies. There is a brotherhood in arms between us and our friends of the United States. There is complete confidence in the Supreme Commander, General Eisenhower, and his lieutenants, and also in the commander of the Expeditionary Force, General Montgomery. The ardour and spirit of the troops, as I saw myself, embarking in these last few days was splendid to witness. Nothing that equipment, science, or forethought could do has been neglected. . . .'

Churchill and de Gaulle
at the tomb of the
Unknown Soldier in
Paris on 11 November
1944.

Paris and Athens

Following the D-Day landings the Allied cause moved from strength to strength. In the east the Red Army broke through the German front line, and on 23 August 1944 the Germans were driven from Paris.

In August Churchill visited the British front line in Italy. Then, on 10 September, he returned to Quebec, where he discussed, with Roosevelt, the completion of the war in Europe, and plans to defeat Japan. While the two leaders talked, units of the United States army fought their way into Germany itself.

In October Churchill was once more in Moscow, for discussions with Stalin; in November he was in France visiting Paris, and the French front line in the Vosges; and in December he flew to Athens, where British troops had been fighting against the Greek communist forces, in order to try to reconcile the warring factions.

Churchill in Athens in December 1944; with him are the Greek Archbishop Damaskinos and (far right) Anthony Eden; whilst this photograph was being taken, there was continued shooting in nearby streets.

Yalta

With the German armies everywhere in retreat, Churchill now faced one of the hardest tests of his career, the negotiations with Stalin about the future frontiers of Europe. To this end, he travelled to Yalta, on the Black Sea, in February 1945, together with Roosevelt. Early on in the discussions, Churchill felt that the Western bargaining position was much weakened, when Roosevelt declared that after the war the United States would take all steps to preserve peace, 'but not at the expense of keeping a large army in Europe'.

Churchill told Stalin and Roosevelt: 'I must say that never in this war have I felt the responsibility weigh so heavily on me, even in the darkest hours, as now during this conference', and he went on to tell the two leaders: 'Do not let us under-estimate the difficulties.

Nations, comrades in arms, have in the past drifted apart within five or ten years of war. Thus toiling millions have followed a vicious circle, falling into the pit, and then by their sacrifices raising themselves up again. We now have a chance of avoiding the errors of previous generations and of making a sure peace. People cry out for peace and joy. Will the families be reunited? Will the warrior come home? Will the shattered dwellings be rebuilt? Will the toiler see his home? To defend one's shattered country is glorious, but there are greater conquests before us. Before us lies the realization of the dream of the poor – that they shall live in peace, protected by our invincible power from aggression and evil.'

Churchill, Roosevelt and Stalin at Yalta.

'Most immediate'

52

Admiralty to F.O. Narvik.   Most immediate.

     Begins.   First Lord to Lord Cork, personal and private.

     Should you consider that situation is being mishandled it is your duty to report either to me personally or to Admiralty upon ~~the situation~~ it and what you would do yourself, (stop).   You should of course inform the General ~~either taking actions~~ of the action you have taken, so that he will have an opportunity of expressing his views to the War Office.

WM

17. 4

One of Churchill's famous war directives 'Action this day'; he himself has added in red ink 'Most immediate'.

Crossing the Rhine

On his return from Yalta, Churchill flew first to Greece, and then to Egypt, before returning to England.

Five weeks later he was travelling again, this time to watch the Allied forces cross the Rhine. For two days he stayed at Montgomery's headquarters, watching the airborne troops fly eastwards; then he himself crossed the Rhine, and for half an hour walked about in the sunshine on the eastern shore.

Shortly after Churchill's return from the front, President Roosevelt died. On hearing the news, Churchill wrote, 'I felt as if I had been struck a physical blow. My relations with this shining personality had played so large a part in the long, terrible years we had worked together. Now they had come to an end, and I was overpowered by a sense of deep and irreparable loss.'

Churchill picnics with the United States 9th Army on 24 March 1945 after visiting the Siegfried Line and the former German 'citadel' fortress of Jülich.

FACING PAGE Churchill crossing the Rhine on 25 March 1945, accompanied by British and United States generals and war correspondents.

158

On 26 March 1945, while still in Germany, Churchill wrote this message in Montgomery's notebook; Montgomery himself has added 'Germany!' in red ink.

The message reads:
Chapter IX
The Rhine and all its fortress lines
lie behind the 21st Group of Armies.
Once again they have been the hinge
upon which massive gates revolved.
Once again they have proved that
physical barriers are vain without
the means and spirit to hold them.

A beaten army not long ago Master of
Europe retreats before its pursuers. The
goal is not long to be denied to them
who have come so far and fought so well
under proud and faithful leadership.

Forward all on wings of flame
to final Victory.

1945/Winston S. Churchill   Mar. 26'

The German Surrender

On 30 April 1945, as the Red Army advanced through the suburbs of Berlin, Hitler committed suicide. A week later, the German Chief of Staff signed the German surrender at General Eisenhower's headquarters in France.

Churchill's wartime travels were at an end. Throughout his journeyings, he had travelled with his own map room, able to follow from day to day each phase of the military, air and sea struggle. The organizer of the map room was Captain Richard Pim, who calculated that Churchill had travelled more than 125,000 miles on his wartime missions, and had spent more than 800 hours at sea, and 350 hours in the air.

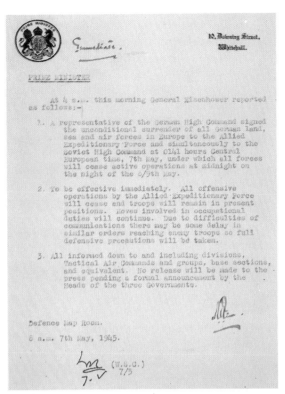

RIGHT Churchill learns the news of the German surrender; he has initialled the message 'WSC' with the date, 7 May 1945.

BELOW Churchill in the Cabinet Room.

Victory and Defeat

Following the defeat of Germany, but before the defeat of Japan, Britain was plunged into an election campaign. Churchill's work, however, was dominated by the preparations for a final conference of the Allied leaders, to be held at Potsdam.

After an election tour that was more like a triumphal progress, Churchill flew to St Jean de Luz, for a brief painting holiday, before flying on to the Potsdam conference, where he discussed the future of Europe with Stalin, and with the new President of the United States, Harry S. Truman.

Flying back to Britain while the conference was still in session, Churchill learned that the Conservative Party had been defeated at the polls. 'The decision of the British people', he declared in a radio broadcast, 'has been recorded in the votes counted today. I have therefore laid down the charge which was placed upon me in darker times.'

BELOW During his visit to Berlin in July 1945, Churchill went to see the ruins of Hitler's Chancellery; here, he turns away from the spot where Hitler's body was burnt, after the Führer had shot himself three months before.

FACING PAGE Churchill sketched by Margaret Nairn as he set up his easel at St Jean de Luz, on the French side of the Pyrenees; he signed her sketch 'Winston S. Churchill, 1945'.

Winston S. Churchill
1925

163

8

Elder Statesman 1945-1965

With the Conservative Party's election defeat in 1945, Churchill became Leader of the Opposition. He was nearly sixty-nine years old, and had put enormous energies into his wartime task. Now he was an elder statesman, honoured by many nations, cities and universities. But he was distressed by the Soviet domination of eastern Europe, and by the division of Europe into two facing blocs, divided by the Iron Curtain. 'I do not believe that Soviet Russia desires war', he declared in 1946. 'What they desire is the fruits of war and the indefinite expansion of their power and doctrines.'

While in opposition, Churchill continued to travel, and to paint. He also embarked upon a six-volume history of the Second World War, and on a series of speeches, both in Britain and Europe, in favour of the unity of western Europe.

In 1951 Churchill became Prime Minister for the second time. In 1954 he visited the United States, where Eisenhower, his wartime colleague-in-arms, was now President. In 1953 he received the Order of the Garter, becoming 'Sir' Winston, and in 1955 he resigned from the Premiership.

In retirement, Churchill continued both to write, and to paint. In 1958 he completed his four-volume *History of the English Speaking Peoples*, which he had begun more than twenty years before, and for which he was awarded the Nobel Prize for Literature.

Churchill died in London on 24 January 1965, at the age of ninety. Two years earlier, in proclaiming him an Honorary Citizen of the United States, John F. Kennedy declared: 'The record of his triumphant passage will inspire free hearts all over the globe.'

Warnings and Forebodings

In the spring of 1946, less than a year after the defeat of Germany, Churchill returned to the United States. There, he made several speeches of warning and concern. At the University of Miami on 26 February he stressed the need for education, and urged 'a generous and comprehending outlook upon the human story with all its sadness and with all its unquenchable hope'. At Fulton, Missouri, on 5 March, he spoke of the 'Iron Curtain', and of the imposition of 'police government' in eastern Europe; 'This is certainly not the liberated Europe we fought to build up', he declared. 'Nor is it one which contains the essentials of permanent peace.' And in New York on 15 March, he spoke of 'the curse of war, and the darker curse of tyranny'.

BELOW Churchill and Eisenhower at Williamsburg, Virginia on 8 March 1946 during Churchill's United States speaking tour.

FACING PAGE Churchill addressing Americans at the Waldorf-Astoria Hotel, New York, on 15 March 1946.

Towards a United Europe

In 1946 Churchill travelled to the Netherlands, to France, to Switzerland and to Belgium, receiving honours, addressing Parliaments, and speaking of the future. Wherever he went, he urged the need to uphold democracy. In Zürich, on 19 September, he spoke of the 'tragedy' of a divided Europe, and declared: 'We must build a kind of United States of Europe. In this way only will hundreds of millions of toilers be able to regain the simple joys and hopes which make life worth living. The process is simple. All that is needed is the resolve of hundreds of millions of men and women to do right instead of wrong and gain as their reward blessing instead of cursing.'

FACING PAGE Churchill at a reception in Belgium during his European tour; with him is his daughter Mary.

BELOW Churchill with Robert Schuman, French Minister of Finance, riding through the city of Metz on Bastille Day, 1946.

struggle, and amid all other preoccupations we viewed its changing fortunes day by day with hope or with apprehension according to the mood of the moment.

The scale of U-boat operations, the increasing toll we exacted from them and the changing shipping position arising from our losses at sea and the gains from new construction, are best understood from the graphs shown in the Appendix to this chapter and the reader would do well to study them with care. Until the end of 1942, despite our best efforts, the shipping losses by U-boats alone continued to exceed ominously the rate of replacement, and to these had to be added the losses from other causes. Unless this state of affairs could be reversed the ultimate destruction of Allied shipping as an effective instrument of war was inevitable. We studied the rising curves of losses and replacement with grave anxiety and pinned our faith on the immense shipbuilding programme which the United States had launched on entering the war. By the beginning of 1943 the first fruits of this were becoming apparent, the curve of new tonnage was rising sharply and the curve of losses showed a welcome decline. Before that year ended the soaring curve of new tonnage at last surpassed the losses at sea from all causes and went on to achieve, by the end of the war, the staggering figure of 45 million tons, or more than twice the entire tonnage of the British Mercantile Marine at the beginning of the war. Against this however must be set the total Allied loss amounting to $23\frac{1}{2}$ million tons.

In the U-boat war the second quarter of 1943 proved to be the decisive phase. During these few months seventy-three German U-boats were destroyed, nearly twice as many as in any previous equivalent period, and furthermore for the first time, U-boat losses exceeded the rate of replacement. These two events, appreciable only through the medium of curves compiled with the utmost care from all available statistics, were most important milestones along the hard road to victory. There was one more milestone later on when the number of U-boats sunk actually exceeded the number of merchant ships sunk in all the Atlantic, but that happy state of affairs was still far in the future.

In an earlier chapter we saw how Admiral Doenitz, finding the coast of the United States no longer so profitable as it had been switched the attack to new hunting grounds. In August he was particularly active near Trinidad and the north coast of Brazil where the most attractive targets offered, including the ships carrying bauxite to the United States for the vital aircraft industry and the stream of outward bound ships carrying supplies round the Cape to the Middle East. Other roving U-boats were at work near Freetown and a few ranged as far south as the Cape of Good Hope in search of "soft spots". Eventually they penetrated into the Indian Ocean and the Mozambique Channel where they linked up with the Japanese. These latter movements were in the nature of a reconnaissance and meanwhile the main battle was once more joined along the great convoy routes in the North Atlantic.

Writing the War Memoirs

As soon as the war ended, Churchill began to piece together the material needed to write his war memoirs. He was determined to tell the story of his Premiership as fully as possible, and assembled a team of experts to help him. The leader of the team was Bill Deakin, who before the war had helped Churchill prepare both his biography of Marlborough, and his *History of the English Speaking Peoples.*

The first of the six war volumes was published in 1948, and the sixth in 1954. Each book went through the most detailed checking and counter-checking. Hardly a single line of Churchill's first dictated version survived intact in his own quest for the most meticulous accuracy possible. For more than eight years his assistants worked to follow up each clue and query.

Churchill gave his memoirs a motto:

IN WAR: RESOLUTION
IN DEFEAT: DEFIANCE
IN VICTORY: MAGNANIMITY
IN PEACE: GOODWILL

and he called his final volume *Triumph and Tragedy,* because, as he wrote in 1953, 'the overwhelming victory of the Grand Alliance has failed so far to bring general peace to our anxious world'.

FACING PAGE A draft page of Churchill's war memoirs.

BELOW Churchill's principal assistant on his war memoirs, Bill Deakin, who had previously helped him both on the Marlborough biography and on the *History of the English Speaking Peoples.*

Painter

Between work on the six volumes of his war memoirs, Churchill returned in earnest to his hobby. In the sun of the South of France, he spent happy hours catching in oils the sunlight he loved so well. He painted also at his beloved Chartwell, and on his many travels, to Italy, to Switzerland, and back to Marrakesh.

WINSTON S. CHURCHILL

PAINTING as a Pastime

The American edition of Churchill's *Painting as a Pastime*, which was first published as a magazine article in 1925 and then as a book in 1948. The American edition pictured here was published in 1950.

One of the lakes in front of Chartwell. Churchill
planned and built these lakes, and often made
them the subject of his paintings.

FACING PAGE Churchill painting in the village of Camara de Lobos on the island of Madeira, a photograph taken on 9 January 1950.

BELOW Churchill's studio at Chartwell, the walls of which are adorned with his paintings.

Prime Minister

In 1951 Churchill became Prime Minister for the second time. Once more he visited the United States where he was greeted by President Truman, and where, at the Walter Reed hospital in Washington he met the wounded of the Korean war. The importance of close Anglo-American relations were always uppermost in his mind. Speaking at a dinner given by the English-Speaking Union, he told his audience of the 'unwritten alliance' between Britain and the United States, and declared: 'It is an alliance far closer in fact than many which exist in writing. It is a treaty with more enduring elements than clauses and protocols. We have history, law, philosophy, and literature; we have sentiment and common interest; we have language. We are often in agreement on current events and we stand on the same foundation of the supreme realities of the modern world.'

In 1955 Churchill retired; to be succeeded as Prime Minister by Anthony Eden.

President Truman welcoming Churchill on board the Presidential yacht *Williamsburg* on 10 January 1952.

Nine days later, in Washington, Churchill shook
hands with forty-nine wounded veterans of the
Korean war.

Retirement

In retirement, Churchill lived quietly at Chartwell, and at his London house in Hyde Park Gate. He continued to visit France, which he had first visited with his father in 1883, when he was eight years old, and with whose fate and fortune his life had been so sympathetically attuned.

In France, Churchill was always welcomed as a friend, and tears often came to his eyes when he recalled the sufferings of the French people in their wars with Germany. 'The road has been long and terrible', he had told a great gathering at Metz in 1946; 'I am astonished to find myself here at the end of it.'

BELOW At the Matignon Palace in Paris, on 6 November 1958, Churchill received the Croix de la Libération from President de Gaulle.

Churchill with his dog Rufus, looking out over
the Chartwell Lakes.

Old Age

Churchill now spent most of the summer months in the South of France, where he continued to delight in setting up his easel, and painting. While in the South of France in 1958, he celebrated fifty years of marriage. He was eighty-three years old.

FACING PAGE Churchill painting in the South of France.

BELOW On 12 September 1958 Churchill celebrated his golden wedding anniversary at La Capponcina, together with his son Randolph, Clementine Churchill, and Randolph's daughter, Arabella.

In the South of France

During the last ten years of his life, Churchill spent most of his time at Chartwell. But he was still able to visit France, and spent some time at the villa La Pausa, above Menton, where he painted and relaxed. His host there was Emery Reves, who, twenty years before, during Churchill's 'wilderness years' had placed hundreds of Churchill's warning articles in the newspapers of Europe.

Churchill painting at La Pausa.

A view of the French coast near Menton, the
subject of many of Churchill's paintings.

Last Years

In November 1964 Churchill celebrated his ninetieth birthday. And then, on 24 January 1965, he died.

ABOVE A selection from more than 150 of the stamps that were printed to commemorate Churchill's death.

FACING PAGE Churchill at La Pausa, a photograph taken by his painter friend Paul Maze.

Funeral

Churchill's funeral took place in London on 30 January 1965, when his coffin was taken from Westminster Hall, where it had lain in state, to St Paul's Cathedral, for the funeral service. From St Paul's it was taken down to the River Thames; then by launch to Waterloo Station, and finally by train to Oxfordshire, where Churchill was buried, next to his father, mother and brother, at Bladon churchyard, near Blenheim Palace.

FACING PAGE Churchill's coffin leaves St Paul's Cathedral.

BELOW The coffin is taken by barge to Waterloo Station.

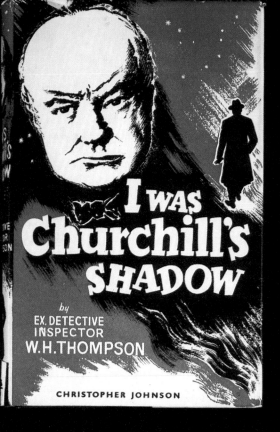

I WAS Churchill's SHADOW

by EX. DETECTIVE INSPECTOR W. H. THOMPSON

CHRISTOPHER JOHNSON

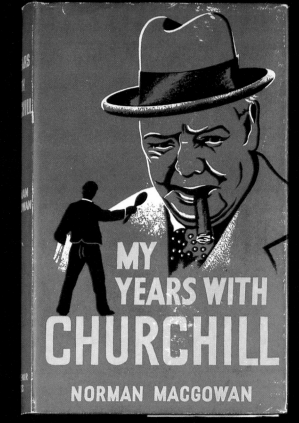

MY YEARS WITH CHURCHILL

NORMAN MACGOWAN

ACTION THIS DAY
WORKING WITH CHURCHILL

ACTION THIS DAY

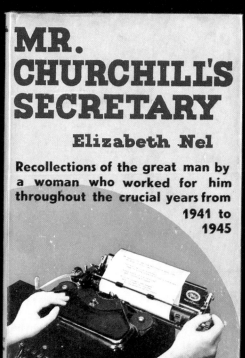

MR. CHURCHILL'S SECRETARY

Elizabeth Nel

Recollections of the great man by a woman who worked for him throughout the crucial years from 1941 to 1945

Churchill Remembered

The first book about Churchill was published in 1905. Since then, several hundred accounts have been written, some by people who worked at his side: political colleagues, fellow officers, research assistants, secretaries – even by his detective. Thousands of his letters have been published in the official biography, begun by his son Randolph and continued by Martin Gilbert.

Two years before Churchill's death, President John F. Kennedy said of him: 'Whenever and wherever tyranny threatened, he has always championed liberty. Facing firmly toward the future, he has never forgotten the past. Serving six monarchs of his native Great Britain, he has served all men's freedom and dignity.

'In the dark days and darker nights when England stood alone – and most men save Englishmen despaired of England's life – he mobilized the English language and sent it into battle. The incandescent quality of his words illuminated the courage of his countrymen.

'Indifferent himself to danger, he wept over the sorrows of others. A child of the House of Commons, he became its father. Accustomed to the hardships of battle, he had no distaste for pleasure.

'Now his stately ship of life, having weathered the severest storms of a troubled century, is anchored in tranquil waters, proof that courage and faith and zest for freedom are truly indestructible. The record of his triumphant passage will inspire free hearts all over the globe.

'By adding his name to our rolls, we mean to honor him – but his acceptance honors us far more. For no statement or proclamation can enrich his name now – the name Sir Winston Churchill is already a legend.'

FACING PAGE Four of the many hundreds of books written by those who had worked with Churchill, or known him, during the many years of his political life.

In these pages we have seen something of the range and variety of Churchill's career. We have seen him at work, and at play. He was a man of infinite variety, of great energy, and of forceful opinions. But he never feared the telling of his own story. 'The truth is incontrovertible', he said. 'Panic may resent it; ignorance may deride it; malice may distort it, but there it is.'

ᕯᕯ Illustration ᕯᕯ Acknowledgments

≫ Index ≪